D1486468

# DUTY AND DISCERNMENT

# DUTY AND DISCERNMENT

*Edited by G. R. Dunstan*

SCM PRESS LTD

Chapter 4 reprinted from *Theology* LXVIII, June 1965
Chapters 1–3 and 6–11 reprinted from *Theology* LXXVI, 1973
Chapter 5 reprinted from *Jus Sacrum: Klaus Mörsdorf zum Geburtstag*, ed. A. Scheuermann and G. May, Verlag Ferdinand Schöningh, München-Paderborn-Wien 1969

334  00339  3

First published 1975
by SCM Press Ltd
56 Bloomsbury Street, London
Printed in Great Britain by
Western Printing Services Ltd
Bristol

# Contents

# *Preface*

The papers published in this volume result from an initiative taken by Professor Enda McDonagh and myself some years ago when we invited a small group of scholars to meet and discuss whether there exists a common ground on which Christians of different confessions could now build a moral theology, or begin to express something like a common Christian mind on ethical questions which they all encounter. Inevitably in such a group, meeting intermittently over a span of years, the question set is lost in the pursuit. Our method was to discuss, to assign subjects to members particularly competent to write on them, to circulate their papers for further discussion, and then to leave each writer free to finish his paper as he would, and to accept personal responsibility for it. When the group turned to consider the natural law tradition as a possible common ground, it found that the necessary questions had already been formulated by the late G. F. Woods in an article, 'Natural Law and Christian Ethics', published in *Theology* LXVIII, in June 1965. That paper is reprinted here, by kind permission of his executors, with two comments from members of the group. After some delay, during which some papers prepared and discussed by us were published elsewhere, most of those remaining were published in sequence in *Theology* LXXVI, during the year 1973. A generous initiative from the Editor of the SCM Press enables us to bring them together within a book. We are indebted to the SPCK, the publisher of *Theology*, for permission to reprint the articles which have already appeared in that journal, and similarly to the editors (A. Scheuermann and G. May) and publisher (Verlag Ferdinand Schoeningh, München-Paderborn-Wien) of *Jus Sacrum*, in which Enda McDonagh's paper, 'The Natural Law and the Law of Christ' was published in 1969.

The work, though unfinished, was well conceived. It is firmly rooted in the philosophical tradition by the contributions of Lady Oppenheimer, Mr Cupitt and Professor Owen; in the disciplines of the exegesis of Holy Scripture by Dr Lindars; in the Roman Catholic tradition by Professor McDonagh and in the Reformed tradition by Professor Whyte; in the discipline of sociology by Professor Martin. It is regretted that plans to attempt a corporate ethical judgment on one or two particular moral issues – revolution was chosen at first – had to be deferred, because external demands on some of our members made it impossible for them to meet regularly enough to keep momentum. Perhaps now, eight years after our beginning, there would be no need to mount such a self-conscious oecumenical attempt; what we then set out to do, at least on 'practical issues', people are now doing all the time. And for that at least we may be profoundly thankful.

*King's College*                                          G. R. DUNSTAN
*London*

# Contributors

DON CUPITT is a Fellow and Dean of Emmanuel College, Cambridge.

BARNABAS LINDARS is a member of the Society of St Francis and a Lecturer in Divinity in the University of Cambridge.

ENDA McDONAGH is Professor of Moral Theology and Dean of Studies at St Patrick's College, Maynooth.

DAVID MARTIN is Professor of Sociology at the London School of Economics and Political Science.

LADY OPPENHEIMER writes on philosophical theology and ethics.

HUW PARRI OWEN is Professor of Christian Doctrine at King's College, London.

JAMES WHYTE is Professor of Practical Theology and Christian Ethics in the University of St Andrews.

GEORGE WOODS was a Fellow of Downing College, Cambridge, then Professor of Divinity at King's College, London. He died in 1966.

# I

# Some Philosophical Problems in Christian Ethics

## HUW PARRI OWEN

This paper is intended merely as a brief survey. I have chosen six topics that seem to me to constitute the main philosophical problems confronting Christian moralists today.

## I

My first topic is a problem of definition. What do we mean by 'Christian Ethics'? If we point simply to the New Testament our definition is too narrow. If we include all the moral reflections that have been produced by all Christian writers our definition is far too wide. If we seek to curtail our scope by selecting some writers as normative we shall probably disagree over our selection and our interpretation of 'norm'.

Faced with these difficulties someone might suggest that 'Christian Ethics' should mean (without any antecedent reference to any document) a corpus of ethical principles and precepts which are peculiarly Christian (that is, which are found in Christian, but not non-Christian, literature). However, it is very hard to construct such a corpus. It is well known that there is *some* parallel (often an exact one) in Jewish and Graeco-Roman literature to almost every moral maxim of the New Testament. A modification might then be introduced. 'Let us look', it might be said, 'for a principle that, though it is not exclusively Christian, possesses an importance in Christian accounts of the moral life that it does not possess in non-Christian ones.' The obvious candidate is 'love' (*agape, caritas*); for this is central in the teaching of the New Testament and of such widely acknowledged doctors of the church as Augustine and Aquinas. Yet whether love alone can furnish a basis for Christian judgment and action is a keenly debated question to which I shall recur. Meanwhile let us note that Augustine and Aquinas certainly did not hold that love, in fulfilling other virtues, superseded them. Moreover, in the fourth gospel and I John our love for our neighbour is derived from God's love for us and our love for him.

In view of the last point some of us might feel inclined to locate the distinctive nature of Christian ethics – its differentiating factors – in its religious background (that is, in the Christian doctrines of God, Christ, and human destiny). Christians and non-Christians ('good pagans'), on this view, perform largely the same moral acts with largely the same moral motives and intentions; but the Christian has further, religious, motives and intentions; and these (to borrow a phrase from C. H. Dodd) impart a new 'quality and direction' to those acts which both he and the non-Christian approve and perform.

To the ideas of 'quality' and 'direction' we must add the idea of 'authority'. This is a complex idea which raises many disputable questions. The basis of it is that Christians have a new, supernatural, sanction for their moral code in so far as the latter has been revealed to them as the will of God. And so I come to my second topic.

## II

All Christians, surely, would agree that for them morality consists in (or at least includes) obedience to the will of God. The concept of God's will in this context raises the following problems of which the first and second constitute objections that agnostic philosophers have often urged against a theological interpretation of ethics.

(i) In his *God and Philosophy*[1] A. N. Flew attempts to impale the theist on the horns of this dilemma. Either an action is right because God commands it, or God commands it because it is right; but if we accept the first alternative we substitute sheer power for moral value, and if we accept the second we imply that moral standards are independent of God's will. This, surely, is a false dilemma. God's commands are right because he himself *is* righteousness (as he *is* all his attributes within the simplicity of his self-existent being). Whether the idea of self-existent goodness is meaningful is of course a further, metaphysical, question.

(ii) It has been urged by Nowell-Smith[2] that to regard God as an omnipotent legislator is to adopt an infantile attitude of dependence that is incompatible with moral maturity. This objection too rests on a misunderstanding. We cannot validly hold that X is God's will unless it commends itself to the purely moral insight that he himself has given us. Conversely, God does not desire anything of us that is not compatible with the demands of conscience and the reality of free will. However, the next problem cannot be so easily settled.

(iii) Even if we have grounds for affirming that God is self-existent goodness, how far can we determine the content of his will? Let us take the primary case of *agape*. We can be certain that God is love and that he requires loving dispositions and acts of his creatures. We can also be certain in defining these dispositions in general terms. *Agape* implies 'care', 'concern', and the virtues of mercy, compassion, and 'openness' to the total situation of one's 'neighbour'. Moreover, we need not have any doubt in the vast majority of cases concerning the actions that *agape* demands. Yet there remains a number of cases, especially in the spheres of social and political morality, where the demands of *agape* are far from clear. *Agape* does not *obviously* demand any one answer to all the problems raised by divorce, abortion, and war. In such cases we cannot (in my view) be sure of God's will. But here we must remember the ever-necessary distinction between objective and subjective rightness. Even when we are in doubt concerning what is objectively right (and is thus in accordance with God's will) we need not therefore be in doubt concerning what is subjectively right (and is thus in accordance with it); for subjective rightness consists in following one's conscience; and the one, unvarying, element in God's will for us is that conscience is always to be obeyed.

It may be said that any doubts concerning God's will can be settled by an appeal to one or more of the following media: the Bible, the church, prayer. These, indeed, are means whereby God discloses himself and his will to believers; but they do not infallibly settle doubtful cases. The Bible's 'authority' is notoriously disputable. We do not accept everything ascribed to God's will in the Old Testament. On the contrary, Christians often reject the validity of the ascription simply and solely in the light of those moral criteria which they have in common with non-Christians. Even in the New Testament those precepts of which we can say with certainty and without qualification that they express God's will are so general that they fail to provide any certain solution to our most perplexing problems – problems which the New Testament writers did not (and perhaps could not) envisage. On the church, it is enough to observe that the only church (the Church of Rome) that admits the possibility of an infallible decision in moral matters has not in fact produced one. On prayer, it is enough to observe that, even if we can ever be sure that X is God's answer to our prayers, we cannot be sure that it is a moral answer (a solution to a specifically moral problem) unless it commends itself to the normal, rational, operations of conscience.

(iv) Can we use the concept of God's will as a *criterion* for moral choice? The answer to this question is implied in what I have already said. We cannot use God's 'will' *simpliciter* as a *sufficient* criterion without committing the naturalistic fallacy. We cannot validly appeal to it as an authority unless we interpret it through our moral judgment. We can say that we do X because it is God's will if, and only if, we are also convinced that X is morally desirable. Unless we are thus convinced we cannot recognize X as God's will. X might objectively be God's will; but we could not (subjectively) perceive it as such; and so we could not appeal to God's will as a criterion.

It may be replied that there is one exception to this rule: the teaching of Christ himself. Even if prophets and apostles are fallible, Christ, as the incarnate Word of God, is infallible. He mediates God's will in its absolute purity. Therefore we are both logically and morally obliged to accept his teaching even if we do not see by our own moral insight the truth of what he taught.

This reply is valid on two conditions. First, we should be justified in accepting only a small part of Christ's teaching 'on authority'; for unless we accepted the mass of it through the immediate assent of conscience we should not have adequate grounds for discerning in him the incarnation of God's holy will. Secondly, we could not conscientiously (and so in a manner pleasing to God) obey any of his teaching if it were contrary to the dictates of conscience. We could conscientiously accept his teaching only for matters on which our conscience was uncertain. However, whether there are in fact any elements in the (critically established) teaching of Jesus that can be thus accepted 'on authority' is extremely doubtful.

### III

Philosophers continue to find difficulty in accepting the Christian concepts of sin and grace. The main questions relevant to ethics are these. What are the grounds for supposing that (as the doctrine of original sin asserts) all men are morally corrupt? What are the forms, and what is the extent, of this corruption? What limits does the latter set to the possibility of achieving goodness by moral efforts that are unaided by grace? So far as grace is concerned, we must distinguish between two ways in which it can be conceived. We can think of it either as the 'gracious influence' of God's love in Christ or as a divine power indwelling the soul. The first of these interpretations does not entail a conflict between grace and freedom. But the second interpretation appears to entail one if we affirm that grace operates in the will at the moment of a supposedly free choice. Can we justify the affirmation on the ground that, although it is paradoxical, it is not self-contradictory? These questions are forcefully discussed by W. G. Maclagan in his *The Theological Frontier of Ethics* – a work that, in my experience, is insufficiently studied by both moral and doctrinal theologians.

## IV

I have already introduced my fourth topic – natural law – in stating that the moral content of judgments and acts is to a large extent the same for Christians and non-Christians. There is an increasing interest in this topic today. Yet I believe that the study will not progress without a more rigorous analysis of 'nature', not only in the expression 'natural law', but in the whole context of morality.

## V

The philosophical question that is most frequently discussed by Christian moralists today concerns the place of law and rules in Christian ethics. Here I can make only two general and complementary points. On the one hand antinomianism is manifestly unchristian. Both Jesus and St Paul expressed their moral teaching in the form of law (that is, in the form of principles which possess a categorically imperatival force). On the other hand, moral theologians have constantly admitted the extreme difficulty of formulating *precise* rules of *action* to which there are no conceivable exceptions. Here are two passages from writers of impeccable orthodoxy.

Aquinas wrote:

Disquisitions on general morality are not entirely trustworthy, and the ground becomes more uncertain when one wishes to descend to individual cases in detail. The factors are infinitely variable, and cannot be settled either by art or precedent. Judgment should be left to the people concerned. Each must set himself to act according to the immediate situation and the circumstances involved. The decision may be unerring in the concrete, despite the uneasy debate in the abstract. Nevertheless, the moralist can provide some help and direction in such cases.[3]

The same admission was made in this century by Bishop K. E. Kirk:

We must abandon the hope of reaching universal principles of cast-iron rigidity; for with the limited powers of review and comparison at our disposal the most we are entitled to expect is that we shall attain to a few convictions as to actions which are generally or normally wrong, but which may any of them turn out to be right in exceptional circumstances.[4]

These passages anticipate all that is true in 'situationalist' ethics. Obviously there is a need for further discussion (especially with reference to sexual morality). A useful basis for such a discussion may be found in Paul Ramsey's *Deeds and Rules in Christian Ethics*.[5]

## VI

Recent discussion has brought to the fore the question whether 'love' (*agape*) is in itself a sufficient criterion for Christian conduct. I should maintain that it is insufficient for the following reasons. First, 'love' needs to be defined. Secondly, suppose we define *agape* as 'a determination to seek what is for the good of other people and to answer the claims they make upon us'. We then need a further description of 'good' and 'claims'. Thirdly, we must not forget the traditional contrast between love and justice. Even if we say that justice is a form of love we must, surely, admit that it differs from other forms. Lastly, some moral duties do not involve other people (at least not essentially and directly). Thus I have a duty to develop my talents and to tell the truth even if no one benefits from my self-development or is harmed by my lies. Certainly from the Christian point of view my ultimate duty is to God. Hence the commandment to love God comes before the commandment to love one's neighbour.

Of course, I have not done any more than indicate what I consider to be the main philosophical questions raised by Christian ethics. Also it is obvious that the answers I have given require amplification. No answer is complete unless it takes into account both moral theology and moral philosophy – disciplines that have existed for centuries and of which 'Christian ethics' is a recently born child.

In concluding, I shall comment on the relation, as I see it, between

Christian ethics and moral philosophy. The relation is a complex one, and I can here only offer four observations.[6]

(*a*) As I have just implied, a knowledge of moral philosophy is a prerequisite for tackling the theoretical aspects of Christian ethics. The moral terms that Christians use – such basic terms as right and wrong, good and bad, duty, law, ideal – have been analysed time and again, often with great subtlety and depth, by moral philosophers. To ignore these analyses and proceed *de novo* would be folly. Even if moral philosophy is sometimes unnecessarily arid, and even though its terms acquire new meanings in Christian contexts, it and its near-relative moral theology constitute the school in which the Christian moralist must learn the principles and art of moral theorizing.

(*b*) Many of the fundamental questions studied by moral philosophers are of the utmost importance to Christian ethics although at first sight they may seem to be academic and remote. I shall give two examples. Both have been discussed extensively by British philosophers in this century. The first question is whether it is possible to define moral in non-moral terms. Moore held that it was impossible; that these terms are irreducible and unique; and that any attempt to define them non-morally is an instance of 'the naturalistic fallacy'. I am sure he is right. But my only point now is that this question is as relevant to Christian as it is to non-Christian ethics; for we must all be equally concerned about the status and meaning of our moral language. In particular, if we are going to be theological 'naturalists' we shall have to affirm, with Occam, that X is right solely because God commands it. Yet surely this is an outrageous view; for it would mean that, if God had so ordained, cheating and cruelty would have been right, while honesty and kindness would have been wrong.[7] The second question is whether our moral language is objective or subjective – whether it contains judgments that are true independently of our attitudes or whether it merely expresses the latter. Now, I am myself convinced on grounds of pure reason that objectivism is true and subjectivism is false. But I am no less convinced that subjectivism is not consistent with Christian ethics and theology. Can we really say that the Christian reaction to the Sermon on the Mount is merely one of 'approval', or that when we call God holy we are merely expressing a 'pro-attitude' towards him?[8]

(*c*) Christian attitudes towards the various 'systems' of moral philosophy are bound to vary. Many of these systems are at least partly incompatible with Christianity. Yet we cannot expect agreement on the degree of incompatibility. Thus there is room for difference concerning the extent to which Aristotle's moral teleology or Kant's deontology can be incorporated into a Christian *Weltanschauung*. Even systems (such as Marxist ethics and atheistic existentialism) that are in principle opposed to any theistic interpretation of morality may contain elements to which a Christian moralist can assent.

(*d*) In ethics, no less than in theology, we must preserve the unity of truth. In ethics, no less than in theology, nothing can be true according to revelation if it is false according to reason. Also in ethics, no less than in theology, an unremitting effort to preserve this unity is bound to involve intellectual tension and uncertainty for some Christians to some degree for some of the time.

# 2

# Ought and Is

## HELEN OPPENHEIMER

My starting-point is a dilemma posed by Professor H. P. Owen in a paper discussed between us, from which he has kindly allowed me to quote. Many Christians have either stated, or assumed, or at least hoped, that 'it is possible to infer one's duties from an inspection of one's nature'. Professor Owen therefore enquires if we can

avoid the following antinomy? If we define 'nature' non-morally we shall fall into the fallacy of attempting to deduct 'ought' from 'is' (i.e. a *non-moral* 'is'); but if we define 'nature' (at least partly) in moral terms our appeal to nature as the basis for an ethical inference is logically invalid. Thus the proposition 'the human species naturally seeks its self-preservation' does not entail the proposition 'I ought not to kill Mr Jones'; but if I qualify the first proposition by saying that human life possesses an 'intrinsic worth', or that (in some sense) it imposes a 'claim' on me, I have anticipated my conclusion in my premise, and so I no longer have a ground for inference.

In addressing oneself to this dilemma it is not necessary to be submerged in the 'Naturalistic Fallacy' formulation of it associated with the great name of G. E. Moore, with all the confusing cross-currents of intuitionist ethics and of whether 'good' is a 'simple non-natural quality'. It is clearer for the present purpose to rely upon Hume's classic formulation in *A Treatise of Human Nature*[1] of the illegitimacy of jumping from an 'is' to an 'ought'. This famous passage is still variously received by moralists and philosophers, ranging from Dr R. C. Mortimer who in the *Elements of Moral Theology* appeared to ignore it;[2] via Miss Anscombe who described it[3] as 'sophistical' but as having the merit of making the obvious need exploration; and Professor MacIntyre who raised the question of whether Hume meant what is usually supposed;[4] to Mr Ronald Atkinson who briskly takes it in his stride;[5] and Professor R. M. Hare who enthusiastically commends it:[6] 'The best implement [for weeding out fallacies] is still the old fork invented by Hume.'

In some quarters 'Hume's law' is in danger of becoming a shibboleth, and not unnaturally there has been a reaction against it, a reaction which has gained strength under the nickname of the 'new naturalism'. Why, after all, should an 'ought' not be derived from an 'is'? Of course no element must appear in a conclusion which is nowhere to be gathered from its premises, but this requirement is not peculiar to ethics and no specifically ethical theory can be deduced from it.[7] 'It is not necessary that the evaluative element should "come in whole" so to speak.'[8]

Indeed the whole matter can easily be made to seem a question of how we like to put it. The man in the street or in the pulpit often seems to express himself in a way which assumes a kind of rough-and-ready naturalism: of course it is the facts of the case which determine what we ought to do. On the other hand Professor Hare in the *Concise Encyclopedia of Western Philosophy and Philosophers*[9] seems to define naturalism away, or at least ensure that there will be very few genuine naturalistic theories: 'An ethical theory is naturalistic if, and only if, it holds that moral judgments are equivalent in meaning to statements of non-moral fact.' The naturalist may be forgiven for thinking that Professor Hare has missed the point, and that the question at issue is, to what extent the facts are 'non-moral' after all. If we put enough 'ought' into the 'is' to start with it will be there ready for us to get out again when we need it.

If we do not want to set the two sides against each other, nor to let the question collapse into triviality, we can see it as a matter of, so to speak, philosophical engineering. Somehow or other it is *necessary* to travel from 'is' to 'ought'. If it is not safe to jump, what kind of bridge is available? In her admirable discussion of the Autonomy of Ethics[10] Professor Dorothy Emmet puts the matter in terms such as this and points out that Hume's own 'bridge' was the concept of human interests and passions. She herself gives plenty of examples of 'bridge notions' such as wanting, needing, pleasure, happiness, health, which, she says,[11] 'are capable of bridging what "is" and what "ought to be done" because they can be given a factual content . . . and at the same time needs, interests, desires, etc., generally speaking, carry the implication that we approve of their being satisfied'. In particular the key concept of Role has a foot in both camps,[12] fact and value, for 'a role relation in a social situation has some notion of conduct as appropriate or inappropriate built into its description'.[13]

The use of such bridges can be made clearer by contrast: one can come to appreciate something by being warned against it, and Ronald Atkinson offers such a warning. He is disposed to beware of 'bridge terms' and 'keep fact and value separate'.[14] Having cited some illicit crossings between is and ought he cautions us against the use of words which 'tend to be used ambiguously between fact and value. "Nature", "natural" and "healthy" are among the more notoriously bewitching examples.' Of course one should know what one is at and many moralists need Mr Atkinson's warning: but granted this, is it not the very ambivalence of these terms which makes it possible, with all caution, to link what ought to be with the real world? Certainly the idea of 'value-free facts' is showing some signs of breaking down empirically as well as philosophically.[15] Some sort of thaw seems to be taking place, which betrays itself when people feel free to say 'value-laden' instead of 'value-loaded'.

At this point we may well say, 'So far, so good.' We can resolve Professor Owen's antinomy quite soothingly by saying that it depends which side one wants to emphasize, that it is unsafe to jump or that there are bridges. Unfortunately, of course, the controversy between non-naturalist and naturalist is much more complicated and indeed confusing; and it makes a difference which cannot merely be smoothed over whether one wants to insist that nature as such is neutral and it is for us to build the bridges and put in the values, or whether one sees ordinary natural facts as 'value-laden' and the bridges already there for us to cross.

Professor Hare as the leading 'non-naturalist' of today is by no means denying that it is possible to get from fact to value.[16] His 'bridge notion' is the concept of 'commending': to call something 'good' is not simply to name a quality which in fact it has, but to *do* something, to 'evaluate' it. We evaluate on the basis of factual qualities and so ourselves bridge the gulf between 'is' and 'ought'. This is an attractive theory, especially in view of the *Oxford English Dictionary* definition of 'good': 'The most general adjective of commendation . . .'.[17] If the dictionary-makers, presumably with no Wittgensteinian axe to grind, have given us the use when we asked for the meaning, does it not become exceedingly plausible to say that, sure enough, the meaning of the word 'good' is not some quality which can be taken apart from our use of the word in commending?

But at this point a much less palatable, though evidently integral, aspect of Professor Hare's view comes to the fore: if commending is something we do, it also has to be something we choose to do. If we build the bridges from 'is' to 'ought' we can apparently build them wherever we like. If I decide to commend something highly eccentric, and am prepared in consistency to follow out this choice in all its logical ramifications, nobody has the right to say me nay. Not surprisingly many philosophers have remained unconvinced by this, and it has been vigorously criticized.[18] Here, surely, is the great strength of the 'new naturalism'. Its exponents, especially Miss Anscombe and Mrs Foot, insist with good reason that we cannot arbitrarily take just anything as good or bad, that choosing and wanting require a background so that 'to say "I *merely* want this" without any characterization is to deprive the word of sense'.[19]

To say 'I want a saucer of mud'[20] is to invite the question 'What for?' The answers admittedly may be most various. If I say 'How simply marvellous to have this saucer of mud'[21] it may be because 'There's nothing quite like it for cooling the blood' or because it is the kind of thing one finds about the house when the children are at home or even because it fulfils some kind of strange inarticulate longing. Perhaps there is no logical limit to what people can actually want, but still the naturalist will insist that there are limits to the criteria people can intelligibly adopt.[22] To the naturalist, choice is ultimately grounded in fact. He will not be persuaded that there is nothing either good or bad but commending makes it so; rather, he is convinced that evaluation must somehow depend upon the nature of the case.

To be allowed by philosophers to say something like this again certainly seems refreshing and encouraging to a Christian moralist. Christianity seems to have something to do with the 'objectivity' of morals, with the 'truth' of moral statements, in fact with getting an 'ought' from an 'is'. It is not that one is hankering for the kind of metaphysical or theological naturalism condemned by G. E. Moore[23] or more recently by Professor R. W. Hepburn[24] in which 'good' is defined as what someone called God wants. If 'good' has no meaning in its own right, or worse, if it even remotely appears that the reason for choosing right is that God is watching and will reward or punish, value is being based on fact in a false way. Nor need a Christian moralist have any special interest in maintaining that morality is factual in the sense that somewhere there subsists a realm of values over and above our world of fact: that would only make bridge-building quite unnecessarily difficult. It is rather that a Christian will tend to be sympathetic to any theory which emphasizes that 'the way things are' gives us 'something to go on' morally. Such a theory, so to speak, puts the 'ought' back into the 'is': whether it speaks of some sort of facts as somehow having a 'claim' upon us;[25] or, more on the lines of Bishop Joseph Butler, of what is good for us depending upon the kind of beings we are.

There is a risk, but by no means a necessity, of putting our moral lives into some kind of straitjacket here. There have been Christians who have undoubtedly been prone to make something very limited and limiting of the concept of 'human nature', still more of 'natural law'. From such cramping restrictiveness Professor Hare would deliver us, in his insistence that people can want odd things[26] and be unable to give reasons.[27] The oddness is in the people, not in their use of the word 'good' to commend what, in their oddness, they want.[28] Of course this is true, but it does not abolish the requirement that people's wants must, logically, be linked in certain ways with what Elizabeth Anscombe in *Intention* has called 'desirability characterizations'. Nor does it show that people can choose for themselves what to want except in rather complex and special situations.[29]

The concept of goodness is indeed connected with the concept of choice but the connection is more subtle. We are moral beings because we are choosing beings: not that we choose our morality, but that we are beings with purposes to whom things matter. We are capable of being happy and therefore of being harmed.[30] To say 'I want this because it is bad for me' is not indeed impossible but it is a very specialized and in fashionable jargon 'parasitic' usage.

As human beings, then, we have 'concerns' in a perhaps technical sense of the word in which it almost means 'ends'. We are not merely objects, nor even merely receiving sets for experience, but agents.[31] It is because of the two connected facts that we mind about the experiences we have and that we affect, indeed largely constitute, each other's experiences, that we are *moral* agents. The 'new naturalists' are saying something like this, that 'concern' in this sense is the raw material of morality, that 'good' is bound up with happiness and bad with harm; and surely they are right. Mrs Foot put it very clearly in 1958:[32]

> I do not know what could be meant by saying that it was someone's duty to do something unless there was an attempt to show why it mattered if this sort of thing was not done. . . . How exactly the concepts of harm, advantage, benefit, importance, etc., are related to the different moral concepts, such as rightness, obligation, goodness, duty and virtue, is something that needs the most patient investigation, but that they are so related seems undeniable, and it follows that a man cannot make his own personal decision about the considerations which are to count as evidence in morals.

All this may sound very 'humanist' and utilitarian, but it sorts well with two very strong strains in Christian thought. First, it may happily be linked with the hedonism of authentic Christianity, the 'reward' and 'treasure' themes of the gospels, the recurring emphasis on the conception that 'at thy right hand there is pleasure for evermore'.[33] Secondly, it fits with the traditional natural law theory, which has had a considerable revival lately.[34] Sometimes this has been understood narrowly as if God had promulgated to the human reason precise and detailed rules applicable to all; but it can well be taken more spaciously, that 'human nature' in its variety and untidiness, its vulnerability and concern, its finiteness and its aspirations, has everything to do with what people *ought* to do and be. An anthropologist will look among these aspects for the variety,[35] and a jurist for the vulnerability[36] of human nature, while a theologian will recognize its 'createdness', but these emphases are not incompatible. They can be flexibly combined in a sort of moderate naturalism which in its Christian form presents the matter thus: that God in his wisdom made the human race in such-and-such a way (here a Christian anthropology would have to be spelled out); and in finding and realizing the true pattern of our natures, complex and mysterious as it is and only distinguishable with patience, we are, in the same process, glorifying God and entering the kingdom of heaven. To do 'wrong', on the other hand, is to go against the grain of the universe. So there comes a stage in one's Christian moral thinking in which all paths seem to converge in a broad highway marked out in a set of eighteenth-century sermons preached in the Rolls Chapel by Bishop Butler.

But of course the road goes on and it is not free from troubles for long. The 'new naturalism' has been marching for more than ten years now and the difficulties in its way are becoming apparent. First, but less formidable than it looks, comes the attack of crude relativism. This can be fairly readily beaten off, by allowing for the variety and richness of human nature: of course naturalism is not committed to the naive view that men are alike as peas in a pod and that what is good for one man or one society must always be good for another. There is no reason whatever why inferring 'one's duties from an inspection of one's nature' should be a simple process. If the relativist denies the relevance of human nature to ethics, pointing to the 'completely different moralities' of Nietzsche or the Trobriand Islanders, he can be asked to look again: the superficial content may be different, but the structure of justification recurs. 'It is better to be strong than soft'; 'It is better to be free than orderly'; we may disagree but we can comprehend, and if we could not we should call it insanity, not rival morality. Indeed in many anthropological museums the 'natural law' moralist may wonder if it is such a solecism to take the short way with the relativist, and affirm robustly that some 'ways of life' are actually less suitable to 'human nature' than others.[37]

Be that as it may, the moralist who proposes to derive ethics from nature will evidently have to take a reasonably broad view of 'nature' or resign himself to being dogmatically authoritarian; and the more he broadens his concept of nature to allow for its actual variety and richness, the more he needs a definite conception of 'good for us' and 'bad for us' if he wants to say anything specific at all. If the net is flexible in all directions, no moral fish will be caught.

This is where the difficulties begin to cluster around naturalist ethics. It has to be assumed that we have some reasonably comprehensive notion of what human 'flourishing' is, of what is to count as hurt and harm,[38] and this assumption is hard to substantiate. The temptation is to mention a few paradigm cases and leave the matter there.[39] Of course to inflict torture is to do harm;[40] it is contrary to the whole economy of a human being, just as to pull a plant up by the roots or to whip an animal is a plain case of doing it harm. But when we come to more difficult and controversial situations involving real moral strain the concepts of good and harm and of human flourishing are much less straightforward. Is punishment a case of 'harm'? Are paternalist deprivations of liberty 'good' for people? Can an artist 'flourish' in his garret, or a missionary among lepers,

more than a hostess contentedly entertaining her superficial acquaint-
ances at a cocktail party? How is one to judge whether an orator
with a crowd hanging on his words is doing well? The ethic of
human nature readily becomes an ethic of 'my station and its duties';
but I sometimes have to judge that I ought to get out of my present,
perhaps comfortable, station and into another which will make
different demands. As soon as one hesitates at the accusation of
complacency the need for decision has nosed its way in again. Where
facts fail to yield values one seems to be left after all to choose one's
morality.

A naturalistic ethic is particularly likely to break down over problems of sexual morality, where one can neither read off the answers
from what one understands of human nature, nor put the questions
on one side as peripheral. Granted that in our society at least a broad
framework seems to have been established, plenty of uncertainties
remain, giving scope for choice whether we like it or not. The
monogamous stable family is admittedly the 'normal' unit, but how
much incidental unhappiness is too high a price to pay for its advantages? Is everything outside its sphere simply illegitimate, or is there
to be limited scope for the casual and uncommitted, for 'consenting
adults', for a divorcee to make a fresh start and even for the lady of
easy virtue with a heart of gold? One may extract from the concept
of human nature a conviction that some or all of these are less than
the ideal, but the concept of human nature as such will never tell one
whether such 'aberrations' are harmless or tolerable or when they
have 'got out of hand'. One of the strengths of Mr Atkinson's book
is to make one realize how easy it is to beg these questions[41] rather
than resolve them properly: but must one therefore begin to listen
again to the voice of the non-naturalist who has been saying all this
time, 'You have got to make up your own mind'?

The Christian naturalist will sooner or later pull himself together
here and affirm that, whatever the case may be for the sceptical
naturalist, he is not simply flung back upon his own decisions as if
morality could be after all a matter of individual taste. The decisions
have been made already by God. Human nature is created nature,
and human flourishing is not what happens to feel like flourishing
here and now but what leads into the everlasting flourishing which
will be eternal life. The word 'eschatological' is apt to come in at
this sort of point, for the 'nature' upon which Christian morality is
supposed to depend, the 'is' from which its 'ought' is to be derived,

is an 'eschatological fact', neither abstract and metaphysical nor this-worldly and ephemeral, but somehow both actual and of ultimate significance. If this is too vague, it is not impossible to specify further. Some human concerns, especially personal relationships, have a quality we are disposed to call 'depth' which seems to open a way into a morality which is both truly humane and capable of being projected on to a larger canvas. The total fulfilment of such concerns is what we might call our 'ultimate' concern: we should recognize it, if we achieved it, as the consummation of human flourishing.

This is exhilarating, but it leads straight into fresh difficulties. Suppose we can decide, perhaps with the help of revelation, what morality here and now is conducive to human flourishing in eternity, have we discovered something purely empirical which might have been otherwise? Is our 'ultimate concern' a sort of present to us from the Almighty, who might have made us with no depths at all or with different depths? Is God in the last resort the great Non-naturalist who makes the decisions by which his naturalistic followers can then abide? This would be a kind of converse parody of the suggestion of Bishop Butler that he might be the great Utilitarian.[42]

The 'new naturalist' is able to produce a steadying thought here: the notion of 'conceptual requirements'. It is a particularly useful insight that it may be, for example, part of the concept of a human being that it has just the kind of 'depths' that we find that we have in fact. It hardly makes sense to say that God could have made us with a 'completely different' morality if he had so chosen. Grant a sort of minimum conception of human creatures, say 'bodily finite self-conscious beings living in societies' and a great deal more follows about what would necessarily be 'good' for us. It is not so much that one can 'infer one's duties from an inspection of one's nature' as that one can infer what kind of duty makes sense from a considera-tion of what 'human nature' means. Professor Hampshire has put it extremely clearly:[43]

There is no possibility that a man's family relationships, his knowledge and mental skills, the effects of his actions on his society, his loyalties and friendships, his tendency to tell the truth, his sense of justice, his good faith in keeping contracts, should be dismissed as altogether irrele-vant to his goodness or badness as a human being.

This takes us a good way towards a full-scale naturalistic morality more attractive to a Christian than the non-naturalistic alternative. It is surely a clear conceptual requirement that human beings should inhabit one world and communicate with one another, and that in this world there should be kinds of experience which they like and seek and others which they dislike and avoid; and that these preferences should fall into coherent patterns. Large areas of morality can be plotted from these elementary bases. Instead of talking grandly about human life as possessing an 'intrinsic worth'[44] one learns to say that the concept of human life involves the concepts of damage and benefit, and that the concepts of damage and benefit in their turn involve a schematic morality: so the 'ought' is to be gently, not roughly, drawn from the 'is'.

This takes us a good way, then; but perhaps not far enough. Conceptual requirements can be strong or weak. Probably the most useful one of all for the jurist, the wish to survive, is not quite as strong as one could wish. Both Professor Hart and Mr Lucas are careful to describe it as a *contingent* fact. Extensive areas of law and morality (for instance, nearly all medical ethics) are built upon it, and it is fair to say that it cannot be thought away from human beings in general. Yet the individual who lacks it, whether he has overcome it on Buddhist principle, or lost it in suicidal misery, does not seem to have forfeited his humanity. That a man does not desire to go on having experiences may mean that he will soon cease to be a man but not that he already has ceased; whereas a being who does not care at all what experiences he has for better or worse, or who is not at all in communication with other beings, is hardly to be described as a man.

Morally still more important, but conceptually still weaker, is the requirement that human beings as such want to love and be loved, that is, that among the experiences they mind about are their relationships with each other. It does not appear that Daleks, orcs or devils are a conceptual impossibility, nor is it evident that psychopaths are not human; so maybe our naturalist morality has to begin to give place here to a non-naturalist *choice* of a loving way of life as 'better' than hate or neutrality? Yet a Christian will jib at the suggestion that *God*, as he understands God, 'could' have chosen to make rational purposive creatures to whom the concept of love did not apply; indeed the fact that it looks as if he did permit such creatures in the case of psychopaths is a telling aspect of the problem of evil as an argument against the existence of God. Perhaps it can be granted that the concept of a human being as caring for his fellows and not only for himself can 'carry', so to speak, some apparent exceptions. If we can define human beings as characteristically loving, a much richer morality can be built in as 'conceptually necessary' to the idea of humanity. So far the strongest 'conceptual necessities' have suggested, for instance, that vulnerability requires any ethic to include a ban on attacks, while the need for communication similarly requires a ban on falsehood; and the wish to survive if we may posit it yields the demand to take life and death seriously. If, furthermore, the need for relationship is also part of what constitutes our nature, all sorts of much more interesting and positive 'oughts' are involved in the 'is' of being human.

Even so we have not arrived at a full-blown naturalism. There remain large regions of human life where choice rather than hard fact retains a plausible title to govern our morality. Especially in the area of sexual morality, the moralist tends to find himself sooner or later commending a way of life rather than appealing to inescapable fact. Why for instance should fidelity between husband and wife demand exclusiveness, unlike fidelity between friends or between parent and child? There are utilitarian reasons, but not of a conceptually compelling kind. There remains room for decision here, though the Christian moralist will probably assign the choice to God and deny it to man. And if there is room for decision, then naturalism has worn pretty thin.

Nor can such decision be left for ever safely and inaccessibly in the hands of God. It seems foolish to ask 'In what sense did God choose "right"?' but the question becomes only too practical when scientific possibilities open up, as they are notably doing in this century, of ourselves tinkering with the human nature which God apparently chose to make. In exercising choice here, are we criticizing the Almighty or obeying him by using the freedom he gave us? Some still think birth control impious; many more are understandably shocked at any interference with our genes or our psychological make-up. But neither naturalist nor non-naturalist can decline to make choices sooner or later: the details of morality cannot be read off from the facts even if its structure can. Certainly the concept of 'human nature' gives exceedingly little clue to the proper limits of man's dominion, even when it is backed up by the concept of 'the image of God'. It is not just sentimental or timid of us to hope to remain recognizably the same species as the one into which Christ was incarnate, but this gives us very little to go on even in discussion among ourselves, still less when talking to the unbeliever.

Another way of arriving at essentially the same difficulty is by
becoming involved with the question of what a human being is *for*.
A naturalist is sympathetic to the suggestion that to be a man is, in
Professor Emmet's sense, a Role: a concept with its foot in both
camps of fact and value. He wants, as she puts it,[45] 'to be able to
talk about the "good man" and not only the "good doctor"'; but,
as she points out, this extension bristles with difficulties.

The standing temptation of the naturalist at this stage is to over-
simplify the concept of a 'good man' as if all we had to do were to
produce a straightforward set of criteria as we might for a good
doctor or a good knife.[46] One wants a knife for cutting, or perhaps
as an ornament. One wants a doctor for healing, or perhaps to sign
a certificate. One can therefore specify what qualities are needed.
What does one want a human being for?[47] One begins to talk about
the ends of man, and a Christian moralist is tempted to do so naively.
What does God want a human being for? 'To glorify him and enjoy
him for ever': yes indeed; but how is this to be filled out? If we
assimilate 'a man is for glorifying' to 'a knife is for cutting' we
make 'glorifying' too specific, as if the best man were the best at
playing a harp. 'Best at praying' is less flippant but still will not do,
for it is either impossibly vague, or it means 'saying prayers' and is
not compatible with a recognizably Christian doctrine of this world.
If on the other hand we do not try to find *one* function for man but
make play with a maxim which has been much bandied about in
this whole controversy, *bonum est multiplex*, we are left still asking
what criteria are available for choosing a good man.

God the Creator seems to have no terms of reference, so to speak,
and this divine non-naturalism seems to have to take shape in a
blankly arbitrary doctrine of election. To think of choosing a human
being like choosing a knife may be petty, but it is more inadequate
still to substitute the concept of choosing a card from a pack or playing a 'think of a number' game. This is what is disquieting about
W. B. Yeats's famous dictum, 'Only God, my dear, can love you for
yourself alone and not your yellow hair', or the madrigal quoted by
Professor Hare,[48] 'Love me not for comely grace . . .'. If there are
to be no identifiable criteria, neither does there seem to be anything
on which any love deserving the name can get a purchase. Is it a
worthy love for which 'anything will do'?[49]

But even if we can satisfy ourselves about these difficulties (and
certainly some of them may well seem somewhat beyond the reach

of legitimate human concern) a considerable problem for naturalism remains. Suppose we have some kind of picture of what constitutes 'flourishing' for humankind, what man's role in the universe is. Suppose we can fit man into some kind of kingdom of ends, as diverse as we please but forming one coherent system: what then are we to say about those who, responsibly differing from us, repudiate the whole edifice? Professor Hare can allow for such deep moral disagreements by saying that in the last resort people may just choose differently; but it is more difficult for the naturalist and particularly for the Christian naturalist.

Professor Hare, or from a more explicitly 'humanist' point of view Professor Hepburn,[50] can say that it is up to us to give life what meaning we can. After a complete specification of what a proposed way of life involves, we cannot justify it any further: we must just decide.[51] But suppose that after all the Christian is right in supposing that life objectively 'has' a meaning, is that meaning compulsory? 'We needs must love the highest when we see it' is surely at least contingent if not false, and suddenly we are as far as ever from building a bridge from the 'is' to the 'ought'. What is to be done with the square peg in Heaven, the man who is not interested in the Beatific Vision? 'I imagine to myself, for instance,' wrote A. Clutton Brock in the symposium *Immortality*,[52] 'Henry James in Heaven. If it were the conventional state of blessedness, what a polite but persistent note of interrogation he would sound in it; how he would still labour incessantly to find the phrase that would exactly describe his dislike of it.'

If one cannot convince oneself that ultimate agreement about moral ends among people of goodwill is inevitable, what can one say but 'Compel them to come in'? A Christian has not much room for manoeuvre here, unless he is able to conceive of Heaven as a kind of apotheosis of the open society in which people are free to follow wholly disparate ideals. Compared with such fundamental differences, questions such as 'extra-marital sex' seem like 'little local difficulties'; but to assume that such basic differences could not arise is to assume, not prove, that naturalism is correct. Eventually such an assumption will probably just have to be made, but one should at least know what one is doing. It is not adequate to treat this as merely a practical problem of education, of getting people to want the right things, keeping Hell or annihilation in reserve for the odd misfit. It is *morally* obnoxious to suggest purely practical techniques in answer to the theoretical question of whether in the last resort people can opt out of being human, if 'human' means what Christianity says it does.

Literally, of course, we cannot opt out. 'We cannot get out of being men.'[53] But suppose some people keep on refusing to be satisfied by *any* empirical answer to the question 'What will fulfil man's true nature?' A non-Christian naturalist might allow that such people can elude him if they are willing to pay the price of not using moral language at all. Mrs Foot allows this escape-route for the less general evaluative word 'rude',[54] though she does not proceed to face the question of whether this safety-valve is available for 'good'.[55] But a Christian naturalist cannot afford to count people out of the entire system of being God's children. Somehow he has got to affirm that blessedness will satisfy, 'must' satisfy, all we could possibly need or want, however inadequate any particular person's present conception of such fulfilment may be. 'Thou hast made us for thyself and restless is our heart until it comes to rest in thee.'[56] To 'disagree with God' about what is good is not just imprudent, nor even just wicked, but nonsensical; but it is apparent that the concepts of 'blessedness' and of 'God's will' need further exploration in this context if the Christian moralist is to talk sense even on smaller matters.

This is no sort of conclusion to the problem of how what 'is' can yield an 'ought'. Indeed I cannot claim to have travelled substantially further than a tentative suggestion I made some years ago, that Christian morality is 'compulsory' in the sense in which food is compulsory: 'We shall starve without it';[57] taking this not as a threat but as some kind of 'conceptual necessity'. To fail to love eventually is to put oneself beyond the possibility of fulfilment, not penally but because it destroys one as a human being. More positively, there is a verse of Psalm 17 which, whatever it means in its own right, sounds in its Prayer Book translation uncannily as if it were stating precisely what a Christian moralist needs to affirm: 'When I awake up after thy likeness I shall be satisfied with it.' To reword the problem in a piece of hallowed language taken out of context is not to solve it. What is needful for a solution is somehow to show how the concept of being 'satisfied' could bridge the gap between the empirical concept of 'happiness' and the moral concept of 'fulfilment'.

# 3

# Nature and Morality

## HUW PARRI OWEN

Various Christian and non-Christian thinkers have held that morality is in some sense 'natural', and (more precisely) that there is a 'natural' moral law. My aim in this article is to distinguish between the main ways in which the idea of morality can be related to the idea of nature, and to determine which of these ways are valid. I hope that my analysis (incomplete though it obviously is) will assist both philosophical and theological reflection.

I suggest that there are at least ten ways of relating 'morality' to 'nature'. I shall indicate them without discussing Hume (on 'ought' and 'is') or Moore (on the 'naturalistic fallacy'). But it will become apparent that I agree with most of what these philosophers say.

1. It may be held that nature and goodness are identical. 'Good' *means* 'natural', and 'bad' *means* 'unnatural'. To this view there are three obvious objections. (*a*) If 'good' meant the same as 'natural' it would be otiose. Evaluation would add nothing to description. (*b*) If 'the good' and 'the natural' were identical, all human actions would be good; for all are expressions of human nature. (*c*) By general admission some 'natural' impulses (e.g. envy) are bad.

2. It may be held that it is possible to deduce duties from non-moral facts of human nature. Thus the mere fact that men seek self-preservation entails the statement 'killing is wrong'; or the mere fact that the sexual act (when completed without artificial interference) often leads to conception entails the statement 'contraception is wrong'. Such claims to deduce 'ought' from 'is', values from facts, are invalidated by two elementary reflections. First, there is no logical contradiction in accepting any fact and denying any duty. Secondly, we often feel obliged to oppose natural tendencies, not

only (as I have observed under 1(*c*)) when they are intrinsically evil, but even when they are normally good. Thus while it is normally right to preserve one's life, it is sometimes obligatory to sacrifice it; and so, *mutatis mutandis*, of conception and contraception, as the moral criticism of *Humanae Vitae* has shown.[1]

At this point three comments are necessary.

(*a*) By non-moral facts I mean facts that are not evaluated either by the moralist or by the agents to whose actions he refers. Thus (to take the second of my examples) I am assuming that the sexual act is not already interpreted in moral terms either by the moralist or by the hypothetical agents.

(*b*) Non-moral facts include the whole range of man's psychical, as well as physical, life in so far as the latter is not subject to moral evaluation. Thus they include love and hatred in so far as these are considered, in a morally neutral way, merely as psychical phenomena which on account of their universality can be called 'essentially' human.

(*c*) The impossibility of inferring moral from non-moral facts affects both the form and the content of morality. It affects the form; for no non-moral fact entails the bare categories of moral goodness or obligation. It affects the content; for *a fortiori* no non-moral fact entails the judgment that X or Y is morally valuable or obligatory.

3. It may be held that morality is natural in the sense that nearly all men have some kind of moral sense, and use some kind of moral language.

4. It may be held that morality (or 'the moral consciousness') is a dominant and all-pervasive element in man's nature; for it brings everything within its scope, and judges everything according to its special principles.

5. It may be held that there is universal (or at least widespread) agreement concerning the content of morality; so that one can compile a list of duties that constitute a 'natural' law.

Of these three last propositions (3) is incontestable; but it rests on the assumption that morality is an autonomous function of the *psyche*; and its only use is to show (what is surely not in doubt) that a totally amoral person is a highly abnormal phenomenon. (4) is also incontestable in theory, although it is often denied in practice. A strong case can also be made out for (5). There is much more agreement than is frequently admitted concerning the basis of morality.[2]

6. It may be held that morality has a basis in human nature in the sense that our duties always (or often) correspond to, and are supported by, our natural inclinations. That there is some correspondence is obvious. Thus the duty of benevolence coincides with the fact that most of us at some time are moved by benevolent impulses. People, in other words, sometimes act spontaneously according to moral principles. But they also act against these principles when they are swayed by contrary inclinations. And in every case the judgment that a particular inclination is good (or bad) is distinctive and autonomous.

7. It may be held that although duty cannot be identified with or inferred from nature, 'the natural' is a *criterion* of 'the obligatory' or 'the good'. The good must accord with, and so fulfil, our nature. Conversely, anything which contradicts or thwarts our nature is evil. But this criterion is either vacuous or circular. It is vacuous if it means that there must be some non-moral elements in our nature to which moral judgments apply or which moral acts fulfil. It is circular if it means that duty must satisfy our moral nature, or that it must be in accordance with those physical and mental aspects of our nature of which we morally approve.

The same point can be made with reference to the teleological and moral senses of 'good'. Whenever we affirm of X – an action, a type of character, a social institution, a way of life – that it is teleologically good, our affirmation is morally invalid unless it is based (explicitly or implicitly) on the independent judgment that X is morally good. If we are to avoid the fallacies involved in (1) and (2) above we must interpret the concept of 'that at which we must aim if we are to fulfil our nature' through the concept of 'that at which we ought to aim because it possesses intrinsic moral worth'. We cannot be morally obliged to fulfil any purpose unless we are convinced by a purely moral act of insight or approval that it is morally desirable. The need for such an interpretation of a teleologically hypothetical through a morally categorical imperative was fully recognized by Bishop Butler for whom the moral life was one in which all human activities are subject to the authority of conscience which, in judging what is intrinsically right, enables man to live according to his true nature.

8. It may be held that natural facts mediate (or express) moral claims, and so constitute objects of duty. The basic fact is that of man's sheer humanity. Every man, simply because he is a man, has

a unique dignity or worth that claims our respect and, if necessary, our help.

This linkage between nature and morality in terms of claims is deeply ingrained in our moral language.[3] Thus if a doctor were asked why he rendered first aid to a stranger he found wounded in the street he would (or validly could) reply: 'Because he was a man, and because he was in distress.' Again, if John is asked why he puts himself out to look after his senile and trying father he replies: 'Because he is my father.' Hence we say that those who fail to perceive such moral claims are, not only morally insensitive, but also unnatural and inhuman.

'Nature' can be interpreted in varying degrees of depth. It can include, not merely non-moral facts, but also the claims that these facts mediate. Here I wholly agree with the following words of A. M. Farrer.

'Claimingness' in the moral sense is not an addition to such a list of characteristics as those of being heavy, yellow-haired, malleable, easily led, and consolable with *aqua vitae*. And yet I do not find I wish to deny that the exercise of a claim upon me by my neighbour's existence is in any sense a fact about him, or to say that whatever fact there is lies simply in response on my part.[4]

In other words, I fully admit that we often perceive facts as value-laden and claim-imposing; that the correlation between claims and non-moral facts is sometimes quite particular (as in the duties we owe to our parents and children); and that the correlation gives us an additional ground for calling morality 'natural'. Furthermore (as Farrer points out) Christianity offers a new (perhaps the only satisfactory) explanation of personal claims in its assertion that each person is created, loved, and potentially redeemed by God.

However, we cannot deduce any statement of moral claims from any statement of non-moral fact. When I say that I care for **A** because he is a person in distress, or because he is my father, I cannot mean that there is a logical (or conceptual) contradiction in asserting, on the one hand that this man is in agony or that he is my father, and on the other hand that I intend to ignore him (as there would be a contradiction in asserting 'he is in agony but he feels no pain' or 'he is my father but I am not his son'). When I am asked why I care for my father I must (if I am to reply fully) say: 'Both because he is my father and because I see fatherhood as claim-imposing.' Hence, although we can say that a person who does not perceive these claims is 'unnatural' in the sense that he does not exercise his moral faculties in order to see the full nature of the reality that confronts him, we cannot say that he is irrational in the sense that he fails to grasp an instance of logical entailment.

Although I have put the point in abstract terms, it conforms entirely to common linguistic usage. Let us suppose we want to convince someone of his duty by forging a link between nature and morality. How do we proceed? By recourse to insight. 'Don't you *see*', we say, 'that since she is your mother you ought not to behave like that towards her?' And if he does not 'see', that is the end of the matter.

Admittedly, once we have apprehended claims by a distinctively moral intuition we can attempt to grade them, in terms of their stringency, according to the natural facts through which they are expressed. Yet our grading can never be absolute. Thus although the claims exerted by a parent or child are normally more stringent than those exerted by a friend or stranger, they are not invariably so. It is a platitude that moral enlightenment often consists in emancipation from the restrictive demands of the family or clan.

9. It may be held that since morality is 'natural' to man it is necessary for man's happiness and fulfilment; so that the immoral man (or the man who opts for an inferior form of morality) is bound to be unhappy and unfulfilled.

Certainly if we believe that morality belongs to the essence of man we are bound to hold that a morally imperfect person is incapable of perfect happiness and self-fulfilment. Yet here we encounter two major difficulties. First, in an evil world the aim of the good man can never be perfectly achieved; nor can he find complete happiness (that is, either the fulfilment of his nature or the joy that this fulfilment brings). Secondly, if an immoral man says that he finds his life fulfilled in self-seeking and sensuality, we cannot adduce non-moral data that will prove he is in error. As soon as we try to adduce such data we distort them. One form of distortion is to suggest that the bad man (in spite of appearances and his own judgment) is always *really* miserable, and that the good man (again, in spite of appearances and his own judgment) is always *really* happy – even on the rack.

The only way out of these difficulties is by an appeal to eschatology – to the belief in another life in which virtue and vice will receive a manifest reward in terms of happiness and misery. However, 'nature', in the context of this discussion, normally means the natural structure of *this* world. Moreover, any belief in a future 'reward' as the natural, inevitable, consequence of present action is (as in the case of Kant) a specifically moral demand for rationality in the moral order. The belief could not be entertained, even as a postulate, by an immoral person.

These considerations are especially relevant to *Christian* ethics. As Christians we believe that the teaching and life of Christ represent the fulfilment of human nature. He himself said that those who practised his ideals were 'blessed' or 'happy'. Yet he required complete self-renunciation from his disciples; and he himself died in agony at about the age of thirty. To the epicurean, or even the utilitarian, the claim (if it is truly understood) that the Christ-like life is 'self-fulfilling' is bound to seem nonsense. Even for the Kantian deontologist it is nonsense without the postulation of immortality. In fact the writers of the New Testament are able to present Christ as the fulfilment of our nature and the source of our beatitude because they see his death in the light of his resurrection (and, correspondingly, the spiritual death of his disciples in the light of their eternal hope).

So far I have confined my attention to non-religious ways of relating morality to nature. I have done so because 'natural morality' and 'natural law' are usually taken to signify a body of moral theory and practice that is intelligible apart from religious faith. I come now to the religious interpretation of the concepts I have been examining.

10. It may be said that we can identify 'the moral' with 'what fulfils human nature' if we define human nature in terms of God's will for us (that is, in terms of what he, in creating us, intended us to be). This identification is obviously valid if God is absolute goodness. But it does not attenuate the autonomy of ethics or solve our moral dilemmas. We could not call God good unless we already had a moral sense. Certainly within the order of being this sense, like everything else, has been given us by God; but it is, as he wills it to be, independent within the order of knowing. It is only by a distinctive act of moral insight that we can say that God is good and that we ought to fulfil his intentions for us. Moreover, when we ask *how* we are to fulfil them we can answer only 'by the performance of religious and moral duties'. The religious duties – prayer, worship, and reception of the eucharist – are obvious enough. But what of the

moral ones? Here we are brought back to the problems concerning God's 'will' and 'authority' that I stated in Chapter 1 above.

The most that can be claimed from an ethical standpoint for a theistic interpretation of human nature is that (to use C. H. Dodd's words) it imparts a new quality and direction to the moral life. It imparts a new quality by defining the ideal life in terms of Christ's character. It imparts a new direction by setting all duties in the light of our love for God and our eternal destiny. Yet in neither of these ways does it entail one and only one solution of those moral problems on which Christians as well as non-Christians are conscientiously and intelligently at variance.

There is one further matter of interpretation on which I must comment. One can attempt to relate morality to nature (without committing the 'naturalistic fallacy') in either a subjective or an objective way. According to the first way, to say that a moral principle is natural is to say that one approves of or commends it, and that such commendation or approval is a distinctive activity of human nature. According to the second way, to say that a moral principle is natural is to say that it is an intrinsically authoritative norm of human nature, and that it is discerned by an appropriate insight or intuition.

Arguments in favour of both subjectivism and objectivism can be (and usually are) stated without any reference to the concept of nature. In any case a proper discussion of these arguments would require another essay. I now wish merely to indicate, in relation to my preceding analysis, three reasons for preferring objectivism.

First, one cannot renounce moral objectivity and its corresponding intuition without also renouncing the whole idea of natural law in its traditional sense; for this sense (to quote from a recent summary)

implies that men live surrounded by a pattern of rights and duties whose claims upon them are quite independent of their attitude towards them, and which lay upon them obligations which are binding upon them whether they choose to accept them or not.[5]

Secondly, I fail to see how we can adopt a moral attitude towards – how we can morally prescribe, approve, or commit ourselves to – X unless it *through its own moral nature* merits our attitude. As I. T. Ramsey puts it:

When in speaking of an action as 'good' we commit ourselves to it, are we not recognizing a prior claim which that action makes on us; isn't a commitment always a response to something which is discerned?[6]

Thirdly, subjectivists cannot justify the deontological language which they inevitably wish to retain. Thus W. D. Hudson, having rejected intuitionism, writes as follows. 'Religious moralists, like other kinds of moralist, are committed to a principle of action: We ought to do what conforms to the will of God.'[7] But this statement (which occurs in the last paragraph of the book) leaves two questions unanswered. First, how can I recognize the obligation (to which I 'commit' myself) except by an intellectual intuition? Secondly, how can I be morally obliged or bound by – how can I owe a moral duty to – anything (or anyone, including God) that (or who) does not exert a moral claim upon me?

Of course intuitionism is also exposed to objections. Yet I am convinced that these can be overcome. Thus Hudson, although he admits that 'there are certain duties which the majority of men in all ages or cultures have recognized' (p. 53), disputes the intuitionist's interpretation of these duties on the grounds (stated on pp. 57–63) (*a*) that to say one intuits a duty is simply to say that one *feels* sure of it; (*b*) that 'intuition is indistinguishable in cases where it is ultimately shown to have been mistaken from those in which it is not'; (*c*) that 'if sufficient weight of evidence comes to light, we are always prepared to concede that what we claimed to know by intuition we did not know'; (*d*) that 'there are no *agreed* tests for deciding whether or not a man is morally "blind", as there are for deciding whether or not his eyesight is defective'; and (*e*) that the postulation of objective claims is an unnecessary reification of moral judgments.

On (*a*) it is enough to observe that the intuitionist claims to possess not merely a subjective (non-cognitive) feeling, but also an objective awareness. (*b*) applies equally to sensory experience; for the 'intuition' of a mirage is psychologically indistinguishable from the intuition of real water. (*c*) is obviously relevant to cases in which empirical evidence determines the intuition's truth or falsity; but it does not apply to moral principles if these cannot be deduced from statements of non-moral fact. In reply to (*d*) it is necessary only to observe that since there is no distinctively moral sense corresponding to the sense of sight there *cannot* be a test of moral blindness; and that even in the physical case the independent existence of the objects which the 'seeing' man perceives cannot be logically guaranteed. It must further be noted, first that on points (*c*) and (*d*) moral and religious intuition are on a par, and secondly that although both forms of intuition are non-falsifiable by empirical evidence, both can satisfy criteria, or tests, that are appropriate to their spiritual status.[8] The answer to (e) is that the intuitionist does *not* 'reify' moral judgments; he refers them to an order of moral claims that he apprehends as real.

One other point must be noted. In order to defend the objectivity of moral principles it is not necessary to hold either that they are fully perceived by all men, or that those who do perceive them have an infallible grasp of the manner in which they ought, ideally, to be expressed in every case. On the contrary, there are many reasons for maintaining both that some people have limited moral vision, and that a sure apprehension of moral claims (together with their cognate values) can co-exist with doubt and disagreement concerning their embodiment in unfamiliar or complex situations.

I therefore maintain that there are three invalid, and six valid, ways of relating the idea of morality to the idea of nature. It is invalid to equate 'the good' with 'the natural' *simpliciter*, to deduce duties from non-moral facts of nature, or to use a non-morally interpreted 'nature' as a criterion of moral judgment. But one can validly hold that morality is natural to man; that it is, indeed, an all-determinative element in human nature; and that it is possible to state principles and virtues which can be reasonably regarded as constituting the basic content of a 'natural' moral law. I have furthermore affirmed that natural facts mediate moral claims; that (with the qualifications I stated) morality can be seen as necessary for human happiness; and that (again with the qualifications I stated) we can identify the good with the natural if we define the latter in terms of a nature that is willed by a holy God. I have also given reasons (from the standpoint of the preceding analysis) for preferring an objectivist to a subjectivist interpretation of morality.

I fully admit that a large and varied number of facts are relevant to moral choices. Yet none of them is determinative unless it is morally evaluated. Also I am not asserting that a non-evaluative description of facts is always chronologically prior to an evaluation of them, or that, therefore, the two mental acts are always psychologically distinguishable. Such an assertion would be manifestly false, and contrary to my thesis that we perceive facts as value-laden and claim-imposing. My only point is that the two acts are logically distinct.

It may be thought that I have overstressed the negative part of my

thesis. 'Surely', I can hear an objector say, 'we no longer fall into
the error of equating "the good" with non-evaluated facts of nature,
or supposing that such facts entail (or constitute sufficient criteria
for) moral judgments. *This* much we have learned from Hume and
Moore.' Well-instructed philosophers have doubtless learned it. Yet
the error still persists in both academic and non-academic forms.
Marxist communism implies the equation of 'the good' with 'what
aids the victory of the proletariat'.[9] Evolutionary ethics is still relevant enough to require yet another refutation.[10] Finally, the most
elaborate reformulation of 'natural law' by a living English philo-
sopher rests on a failure to distinguish between a moral, categorical,
imperative and a utilitarian, hypothetical, one. I refer to Hart's
concept of 'social necessity' – a concept which has been criticized
thus by D. J. O'Connor in the last paragraph of a book that is, in my
opinion, the most acute recent discussion of natural law:

> Given these facts, it is necessary, if men are to live together at all, to have
> certain rules protecting their personal safety and property and ensuring
> that degree of mutual forbearance and respect that will make social
> living tolerable. Such are precepts of social morality and the enacted laws
> that guarantee that these rules are, by and large, observed. We might
> add to Hart's list that there are certain facts about human wants and
> satisfactions that make for a limited community of interest. No one likes
> being starved, imprisoned, or otherwise physically ill-used. We have
> certain common sources of pleasure and grief. In spite of the limitations
> of the maxim 'Do as you would be done by', we can act on it to a
> limited degree that is not jeopardized by variations in tastes and interests.
> To this limited extent, we can base a set of social rules on human nature
> as we know it. And, in fact, this is the basis on which social rules are
> laid down. But this is a very much diminished theory of natural law. It
> prescribes no unconditional moral imperatives. It says only: If men are
> to live together and find such living tolerable, there are certain human
> wants, failings, and weaknesses that must be recognized. This is no
> doubt an uncontroversial minimal theory of natural law. But it is un-
> controversial only because the mainspring of morality has been extracted.
> We are given no reason why we ought to act in any particular way. And
> this fact emphasizes once again the difficulty facing any attempt to base
> *morality* on human nature.[11]

C. S. Lewis makes the same point less technically in commenting on
the popular view that morality can be justified in terms of social
self-interest.

> It is perfectly true that safety and happiness can only come from indi-
> viduals, classes, and nations being honest and fair and kind to each

other. It is one of the most important truths in the world. But as an explanation of why we feel as we do about Right and Wrong it just misses the point. If we ask: 'Why ought I to be unselfish?' and you reply 'Because it is good for society', we may then ask 'Why should I care what's good for society except when it happens to pay *me* personally?' and then you will have to say, 'Because you ought to be unselfish' – which simply brings us back to where we started.[12]

The same difficulty emerges on a lesser scale from a book recently written by Herbert McCabe.[13] He dismisses the naturalistic fallacy on the ground that no account of human behaviour can be purely physical. 'To describe an event as a killing', he writes on p. 93, 'is already to describe it as having place in a field of communication and not simply in a gravitational or electro-magnetic field.' This, of course, is true; but it misses the point. To ascertain the intention and circumstances of the killer is one thing; to pass a moral judgment on him is another. In a footnote on the same page McCabe uses the word 'murder' instead of 'killing'; but 'murder' *means* 'an act of killing that is morally illegitimate'; and many acts of killing, while being fully human or personal, are not murderous.

McCabe affirms that it is a mistake to regard morality as a matter of right and wrong, good and bad. It is, he asserts (quoting D. H. Lawrence) what satisfies our deepest (as against our superficial) wants, and what therefore produces an enlargement and enrichment, not a contraction and impoverishment, of our lives.[14] In criticism the following points must be made. First, we often do not want (in any recognizable way) to do the moral thing. Even Christians who possess sanctifying grace and persevere in prayer continue to experience the conflict between duty and desire. Secondly, a want is not a moral want unless it is morally determined. Thus I can want to feed the hungry in order to gain a reputation for altruism. Thirdly, in no instance is 'I want to do X' equivalent to 'I ought to do X'. Yet I can scarcely think that McCabe intends to exclude 'duty' and 'obligation' entirely from Christian moral discourse.

Moreover, even if a person can be brought to see that moral goodness is what he most deeply wants, and even if he finds in it a satisfaction that he finds in nothing else, he still must face the following facts. First (as I have just said) he constantly finds that his desire for goodness is overwhelmed by contrary desires; so that the pain of moral struggle counterbalances the joy which his moments of moral spontaneity produce. Secondly, all his moral efforts are imperilled by the incalculability and sheer evil of the world. Lastly, he has to face the fact of death – his own death and the death of those he loves. It seems to me as obvious as anything can be that these obstacles to moral self-realization can be overcome only by faith in God. Morality fulfils human nature if, and only if, it is illumined and aided by the supernatural grace of Christ.

In conclusion I shall indicate the bearings of this essay on the papers read at the 1968 meeting of the Christian philosophers' group, and published in *Religious Studies*, vol. 5, in 1969. I am pleased to note that W. D. Hudson, although he wishes to ground value in fact, concedes the distinction I made through the example I chose. He admits that there is no contradiction in a man affirming on the one hand that X is his father and on the other hand that he is not concerned for his father's welfare.[15] I also agree with Paul Helm in emphasizing the logical importance of this admission.[16] I further endorse A. D. Galloway's thesis that moral enlightenment and maturity consist in an awareness of the discrepancy between fact and value. 'The problem of the growing child', he writes, 'is not how to associate fact and value, but how to separate his perception of value from his perception of his parents or whoever his "heroes" may be'.[17] Moral growth consists in (*inter alia*) a constant and often painful reassessment of things and persons in the light of experience and reflection. This process should lead (as Galloway urges) to the realization (which is the only final deliverance from idolatry) that God constitutes the only absolute coincidence of fact and value, and so the only unconditioned object of admiration.

# 4

# Natural Law and Christian Ethics

## GEORGE F. WOODS

The purpose of this paper is to open a reconsideration of the relation of natural law to Christian ethics. It consists of questions rather than answers. I ask whether it is now opportune to undertake this reconsideration. I ask what are the major impediments to this undertaking. And I ask whether any progress can be made. I do not mean that these are the only questions which can usefully be asked about the natural law tradition.

The Bishop of Exeter is reported as saying in the Church Assembly on 4 July 1963,

The Church of England is beginning to pay the price for its neglect of, and even contempt for, moral theology during the last two or three hundred years. It is paying the price for an exaggerated exaltation of New Testament ethics at the expense of a Christian ethic which combines with the Gospel ethic the concept of Natural Law. . . . What is urgently needed throughout the whole of Christendom is a reformulation in modern terms of the concept of Natural Law.

This reformulation is opportune today, not only in being a re-affirmation of an element in the Christian ethical tradition, but also in offering a promising starting-point for profitable ethical discussion between Christians and those who no longer profess the Christian tradition. The appeal to natural law is an appeal to reason. It does not demand an acceptance of the Christian revelation. It does not require any submission to the authority of holy scripture or to the authority of the Christian church. In appealing to what is natural to man, there is an appeal to the experience of being human which is congenial to an empirically minded age that is suspicious of any reference to the transcendent. In being a law of human nature, it offers a basis for human morality which is free from the charge of being no more than the habitual law of some limited social group, such as a particular race, nation, class or church. In its universality in space and time it offers a universal basis for morality which all men of sanity ought to accept. When humanity is divided against itself in innumerable ways, the tradition of natural law is plainly worthy of reconsideration by all men, whether they are Christians or not.

The tradition of natural law in the Western church comprises many elements. It is a complex of many beliefs about man, the world, and God. These beliefs are innumerable but the main assertions may be summarized in five affirmations. (i) God is the creator and sustainer of the world. This may be called a natural world in having a nature and a natural law. (ii) The natural world is composed of natural entities, each of which has its own nature and natural law. (iii) Unlike the irrational entities, man is a rational creature with a rational knowledge of his own nature and of the law of his nature. (iv) The natural moral standard for man can be suitably expressed as a law which applies to man in the various situations in which he may find himself. (v) Man is free to follow or to refuse to follow the law of his nature. These five affirmations express, without in any way exhausting, the complexity of the natural law tradition in Christian moral theology. In formulating these propositions, one is acutely conscious that all the words which are used are as elusive as goldfish in a bowl. They are most satisfying when no effort is made to handle them.

It is obvious that this tradition may be accepted or rejected as a whole or in parts, and the acceptance or rejection may in each case be based on many kinds of metaphysical and moral grounds. When the tradition is substantially rejected by one or both parties in an ethical discussion, it is plain that it cannot offer a common basis for their deliberations. They cannot appeal to what is substantially rejected by one or both of those who are seeking agreement by discussion. A formidable number of objections have been made to each of the five affirmations just enumerated. That God is the creator and sustainer of the natural world is widely denied. That the natural world is composed of natural entities, each of which has its own nature and natural law, is more easily said than understood. What is the natural world? Is it a unity in itself or is it no more than a unified view which we naturally take of what we call the natural world? What does the natural world comprise and how does it hold together what it comprises? Can we conceive of the natural world, except in terms which refer primarily to natural entities within the natural world? Are we then perpetually liable to conceive the natural world as itself a natural entity within a more inclusive natural world? In what sense does the natural world possess a nature and a natural law? It is inevitable that when our idea of the natural world is less than clear, our conception of natural law in relation to both irrational and rational entities is less than clear. The loss of confidence in natural theology has led to a loss of confidence in natural law.

The third affirmation that man is a rational creature with a rational knowledge of his own nature and of the law of his nature is open to many similar questions and objections. In what sense is man said to be rational? Does this refer to man's nature before or after the fall of Adam? If the story of the fall of Adam is not accepted, the question still remains whether it is justifiable to think that man is a rational animal. What part is played by heredity and environment in determining what is taken at any period to be the rationality of man? Can the rationality of man be discovered by empirical enquiries or must there be an evaluative judgment upon the empirical facts about the evolution of man which have been collected? What confidence can we place upon any such judgment which is made? Has sufficient time yet elapsed to disclose an essential nature of man which will not be superseded in the course of natural evolution? And does man possess an essential nature or does his nature consist in a capacity perpetually to generate his existence in the process of daily living? If man has a rational insight into the law of his nature, what is seen? What assured and universal content has the natural law for man? If a man has a law of his nature, why ought he to observe it? And does man have a single nature or is he a conjunction of many natures? If so, is this conjunction inexplicable? Or is it his nature to be human only when he rightly uses the system of natures which together constitute what he is? And, if man ought to be natural in the sense of developing according to his nature, in what sense does his nature include the obligation to become what a true man ought to become? How can we conceive of human nature as at once natural, developing, and final? In any case, if he has this rational knowledge of his own nature, he cannot know what to do in particular situations without a sound knowledge of the facts.

These include far more than what he may know by insight about his own nature.

The fourth affirmation is that the natural moral standard for man can be suitably expressed as a law which applies to man in the various situations in which he may find himself. There are many contemporary misgivings about the expression of the moral standard in legal terms. Christians who oppose love to law, and those who reject universal moral laws which admit of no exception, unite in fearing that an acceptance of the natural law tradition may lead to a revival of legalistic moralism. The final affirmation that man is free to follow or to refuse to follow the law of his nature raises the whole unsolved problem of freewill. The conception of natural law in regard to man cannot be the same for those who accept and for those who reject freewill in man because any view of the nature of man must include some view of the moral freedom of man.

It is rather misleading to examine objections to the natural law tradition as though they arose in complete isolation from one another. There can be a general sense of misgiving, amounting to antipathy, which is more than a series of particular criticisms. This general dislike of the tradition lies behind the particular points at which the misgiving is expressed. The discussion has more the character of a conversation between someone who affirms that a man can really only live in London and someone who affirms that a man can really only live in the countryside. The particular points in dispute represent fundamentally different views of what it means to be really alive. A traditional revulsion against the natural law tradition is found for example in many Protestant traditions about the nature of Christian ethics. The claim is that the foundation of Christian ethics is not natural law but Christ. The ethics of the gospel cannot be rightly understood in terms of natural law. The converted Christian is a new creature. As a new creature he has a new insight into the Christian way of life and new power to follow it. He hears and answers his calling. It is an ethic of personal vocation which enables a man to hear and to respond. There is a discontinuity between the old life and the new. It is far more than an unchanged person simply changing his mind and deciding to keep the moral law which he has hitherto not kept. From this standpoint, there are misgivings about the whole temper and structure of the natural law tradition. It is feared that the whole natural law system will conceal the gospel. It is not a doorway into Christian ethics but an unbroken

wall surrounding them. What is valuable in the natural law tradition
can be rightly appreciated only from within the gospel. Christ is the
only key to moral truth.

It is obvious that some of the difficulties encountered in thinking
clearly and distinctly about metaphysical ethics are due to the un-
avoidable limitations of the language used in posing and answering
the questions. 'Natural Law' is not a plain and straightforward
phrase. It is composed of two words used analogically. Each requires
examination. This involves considering the site in which the word
is originally used and then observing its utility as applied analogically
to the new situation which it is supposed to illuminate. To use
analogies which do not illuminate is to throw dust into our own
eyes. From whence do we derive our idea of nature? It comes from
our experience of natural entities being brought to birth. We can
devote our attention to what is born or to the natural process in
which the birth took place. We can think in terms of natural causes
and natural entities. We run into difficulties when we think of
natural entities which do not come into being by natural birth. It is
not illuminating to say that an inorganic entity is a natural entity.
It is not enlightening to say that the natural order is itself natural,
because we do not believe that it came to birth as a natural entity is
born. The course of the natural order is described but not explained
by being called the natural order. To say that a law is natural is not
an explanation of it. A natural law is very unlike anything which is
brought to birth. If the law is said to be natural only in the sense of
being a name for an observed regularity in nature nothing has been
said about its origin or about the way in which it applies to the
natural order. In so far as a natural law expresses what is the case,
little is being disclosed about its claim to express what ought to be
the case. Even if the idea of a natural law were clear, it has only a
limited analogical relevance to what is called a natural *moral* law. It
may be that this is a fundamentally misleading way of thinking
about what we really want to say about the character of the moral
standard. The word 'natural' is depressingly uninformative.

The second word which is used analogically is 'law'. We have
experience of laws which are laid down by the will of those in
authority. Each law is an expression of the will of a lawgiver. A
public law covers a whole range of comparable cases. It would be
intolerable to have a special law for every special case. It follows that
those who believe that what is ultimate is impersonal cannot be

happy in describing the actual or the ideal course of nature as law-abiding. There is no law by which it can abide. No one has laid down anything. And those who believe that ultimate reality has a personal character should realize that we cannot fully interpret its operations in terms drawn from our experience of human law-making. God is far more than an enlarged human lawgiver. When the moral law of nature is interpreted as the law of God, the limits of analogical propriety are being approached. At innumerable points we urgently need a deeper linguistic clarification of the curious phrase 'natural law' as used in the discussion of the relation of natural law and Christian ethics.

When these objections and misgivings are assembled and seriously studied, it is obvious that there is no clear and distinct tradition of natural law in the realm of ethical discussion which means the same for everyone and is accepted by everyone, but we need not be seriously depressed by a recital of some of the objections which have been raised against the natural law tradition. No fundamental affirmation about the world, the soul, or God is exempt from objections. No metaphysical view of the world has yet won universal acceptance. And we need not be completely worried by the fact that human language shows signs of great strain when it is used to make fundamental affirmations. Every word used is being constrained to fulfil a function for which it was never originally designed. Linguistic difficulties are to be expected. There is no need to abandon the effort to rehabilitate the natural law tradition. I think some progress can be made though I do not expect any rapid restatement of the tradition which will win universal acceptance. One line of possible advance is to institute a factual enquiry into the wide areas of agreement about morally admirable acts, habits, attitudes and principles. No one would wish to deny the great variety of moral convictions which have been and are still held by man, but it is unjustifiable to ignore the many points on which there is widespread agreement. Any appeal to facts must be to all the available facts and not only to those which support a particular point of view. There is evidence of moral agreement as well as of disagreement. Fairness and justice are admired in many societies which in other matters are very divergent. Though experienced lawyers may detect many ambiguities and obscurities in the United Nations' Declaration on Human Rights, it does present a remarkable range of moral issues on which agree-ment is professed by a great variety of nations which include members of many races and social traditions. There is a wide measure of agreement about the proper rights of a human being. In our own day, we have the interesting and significant growth of professional codes in Great Britain. The number of these is rapidly increasing. Each represents an agreed standard of judgment which can rightly be expected from members of a particular occupation, profession or vocation. They do not define ideal standards but they describe the kind of things which are or are not done by members of these callings who are worthy of their calling. The fact of these codes shows that those who are intimately engaged in the same kind of work come to recognize standards of work which are widely acknowledged as morally justified. These codes are not the continuation of a long tradition which is imposed by some authority, ecclesiastical or civil. They spring directly from contemporary experience of living in society. It seems very unlikely that these could arise in this way if there was nothing at all in the contention that there is some kind of moral standard which is natural for human nature. And, though psychiatrists can differ widely in their descriptions of an ideal personality, I find that their ideas of a mature, balanced, and wholesome personality are surprisingly similar. This suggests that, despite linguistic and metaphysical problems, there is a considerable agreement about the kind of person a human being should be. A patient study of the areas of moral agreement might promote a more sympathetic reconsideration of the claim that there is some kind of natural norm of human nature.

The only plain achievement of this working paper is to show how much work remains to be done. We must never underrate the manifold problems in any attempt to rehabilitate the tradition of natural law and to reconcile it with the tradition of New Testament ethics. We need far deeper studies of the similarities and the dissimilarities, the continuities and the discontinuities between the two traditions. I cannot see any final compatibility or continuity between natural and revealed ethics, if in the last resort what is said to be contained in revelation is exempt from the scrutiny of reason and conscience and common sense. Despite the obvious limitations and frailties of human reason, I believe that it has an essential place in all genuinely Christian ethical thinking and I hope that there is no ultimate incompatibility between natural ethics and Christian ethics; though I doubt whether this compatibility can be fully seen in this present life.

# A Comment from the Reformed Tradition

## JAMES WHYTE

*Naturam expelles furca tamen usque recurret.* Natural law, too, has
an uncanny habit of coming back, even into the places from which
it had been expelled. If the Reformed tradition appears to have
neglected or expelled natural law, it is because it has found little use
for it in the explication of the ethic of the Christian community, not
because it denies the existence of a natural morality outside of the
Christian faith.

Both Luther and Calvin use the term 'natural law'. Calvin
denounces as 'dangerous and seditious' the opinion that no state is
well constituted 'which neglects the polity of Moses and is governed
by the common laws of nations'.[1]

Equity, being natural, is the same for all mankind; and consequently all
laws, on every subject, ought to have the same equity for their end. . . .
Now as it is certain that the law of God, which we call the moral law, is
no other than a declaration of natural law, and of that conscience which
has been engraven by God on the minds of men, the whole rule of this
equity of which we now speak is prescribed in it.[2]

Luther held that in the kingdom of this world God has subjected
all things to reason. He can therefore speak of the 'natural law' and
the 'natural light' by which men know how to order the affairs of
this world. For Luther, just as there is no *Christian* way of building
bridges so there is no *Christian* way of running a state. 'It is not
necessary for the Emperor to be holy; he does not need to be a
Christian in order to rule. It is sufficient for the Emperor to possess
reason.'[3]

Neither Luther nor Calvin shows any interest in the sophisticated
teleological argument on which Thomas Aquinas founded his
doctrine of natural law. For Luther it is simply 'reason'; for Calvin

it is part of natural revelation, i.e. 'the conscience engraven by God on the minds of men'. The question of the scope of this natural law, whether it includes both tables of the law or only the second,[4] and of the Christian's relationship to it, are matters on which the Reformed and Lutheran traditions differ. But both differ from the Thomist tradition in seeing this natural morality within the common law of nations as a much more direct expression of the rule of God than is found in the philosophical formulations of the traditional doctrine of natural law.

G. F. Woods is right to point out that both parts of the term 'natural law' raise problems for the modern mind. It is doubtful whether the use of the legal model or the use of the ambiguous term 'natural' are helpful today in interpreting moral reality. Yet it is important to try to understand what elements in man's moral awareness have given rise in the past to the doctrine of natural law, to ask whether these same elements continue to exist today, and if so how they are to be understood.

The doctrine of natural law posits some *sensus communis moralis*,[5] the possibility of some measure of agreement about moral matters among men, irrespective of their particular religious beliefs. The doctrine as traditionally elaborated in Christian theology – in the five affirmations which G. F. Woods discerns – is the theory by which some Christians have sought to explain this moral consensus of mankind, and by which they have justified their expectation of moral agreement among men. (It appears to me that this is an important part of the situation; we expect men to see that certain things are right and wrong, and for breaches of this 'law' we consider them worthy of *blame*, whatever their beliefs. Ignorance of this law is no excuse.) Only within a 'Christendom' situation, however, could it be expected that the traditional Christian theory would commend an agreement anything like as wide as the consensus itself. In fact, the traditional theory had the effect of bringing natural law within the control of the church, and the Church of Rome to this day claims to be the authoritative interpreter of the natural law.[6] As long ago as Grotius an alternative foundation for natural law *etsi Deus non daretur* was sought by the jurists.

Today the traditional theological foundation of natural law, as Woods has shown, is open to question at many points. Not only can it not provide a basis of agreement between Christian and non-Christian, it cannot provide a basis of agreement among Christians.

Against the possibility of the rehabilitation of the tradition today we have to set at least these three considerations.

(i) The relativism of our modern culture. Social anthropology and sociology have made us see our Western tradition as only one among many; there is scarcely any moral principle which can be found to have universal acceptance. St Thomas was, of course, aware of this problem, but he considered that deviations from natural law were due to the perversion of reason by evil habit – as, for example, the fact observed by Julius Caesar that theft was not considered wrong among the German tribes. Moreover, both Thomas and Calvin recognized that the particular determinations of natural law were different in different situations or different countries. Modern relativism cannot however be so easily dismissed. We are led to see that not only the particular applications of moral law, but the whole structure of the moral values of a society is relative to the needs of its social structure and the demands of its physical environment.

(ii) The unprecedented expansion of knowledge and the constantly accelerating progress of human invention and competence. When the limits of the *possible* are removed, it is hard to retain the limits on the *permissible*. 'I can, therefore I ought' becomes the maxim of the modern technologist. New moral problems arise for which there seems to be no traditional guidance, and the Promethean pride which is the secret of man's scientific achievement is also the attitude which he takes to his moral dilemmas. The concept of natural law appears to belong to the static medieval world, rather than to the modern world with its pronounced dynamism. Even human nature is no longer seen as something fixed and given; man himself is part of the developing process.

(iii) The revolutionary protests against the traditional values of Western civilization. On the one hand there are those who believe that the traditional values have been used always as a smoke-screen to cover injustice, that the use of reason has been to rationalize in moral terms the self-interest of the dominant group in society. On the other hand (and this is a protest as much against modern technology as against traditional morality) there are those who exalt the values of the feelings – spontaneity, integrity, generosity, openness – over against the values of the reason, who are concerned with persons and relationships as against institutions and order. Both movements today have the negativity of protest, and may not produce great moral fruit. The oppression of the new collective may well be worse than that of the old dominant class; and the romanticism of pure feeling may well pass over into vitalism and nihilism. Nevertheless, the elements of truth in the protest should make us critical of any reformulation which ignores them.

In the light of these considerations, what can be said in favour of some form of 'natural law'?

(i) We must take seriously the relativism of modern culture and accept the fact that many of our cherished moral attitudes and assumptions are by no means self-evident, but relate to a particular historical tradition, and the maintenance of a particular form of society. Nevertheless it becomes a matter of practical importance for us today to find what moral consensus exists, so that in our pluralistic society men of different faiths and of none can co-operate for common ends. I share Woods's optimism about this. The claim that without religion morality is impossible has been made by some Reformed theologians, but it does not seem to be a part of the Reformed tradition. Perhaps it is pressed more by preachers than by theologians. The humanist has a right to resist a claim which is so patently false. 'There is no ground for saying that without religion morality is impossible. Every society has a morality in the sense of a set of views about how its members should and should not behave.'[7] I am inclined to agree with H. L. A. Hart that the basic fact at the root of the moral consensus of mankind is the fact that man must survive. Man is a social animal; survival has always meant some form of co-operation in society, and this has involved some form of order, of family organization, of property right, of truthfulness and trust – that is, *some* form of 'Thou shalt not kill, thou shalt not commit adultery, thou shalt not steal, thou shalt not bear false witness.' Human society of any kind requires that actions destructive of society be disapproved and any particular society will disapprove actions destructive of that particular form of society.

(ii) One result of the vast expansions of knowledge and of human competence in our time is that moral attitudes which formerly made for social peace and order and for the survival of a society no longer always do so; and some, if persevered in, make instead for its destruction. For example, the traditional sex ethic of Western society was designed, among other things, to guard fertility. For this reason birth control and various forms of sexual deviation were condemned, and in the hierarchy of sexual sins any act (even masturbation) which did not carry with it the possibility of procreation became a more heinous sin than simple fornication. In a situation in which, by reason of disease, etc., the population was static, fertility had to be safeguarded. But in a situation such as ours, in which the human race is threatened with destruction simply from the ever-accelerating increase of its own numbers, high fertility is anti-social and highly irresponsible. Similarly, in a world which requires global planning and thinking, and over which the threat of nuclear war is always hanging, the virtue of patriotism in its traditional form may be a dangerous form of madness. So we may criticize the ethical attitudes of society because, in a changed situation, they have become suicidal, and the survival of society is threatened by them.

We also, however, criticize on other grounds, and here we go beyond the criterion of survival. We may criticize a society which makes what seems to be a successful adaptation to a new situation if in process of securing its survival it destroys its *humanity*. Certain societies appear to be 'dead ends' (e.g. ancient Sparta) because there is no future in them, no possibility of human development and growth. That is to say, at some point we operate, not with a simple criterion of what is necessary to prevent social disintegration, but with some conception of what makes for what Lady Oppenheimer has called 'human flourishing', or what Fr Schillebeeckx calls what is 'worthy of man'.[8] It is the spelling out of such a criterion that is being asked of us by many who are involved in technological advance and social planning, who are aware that cost-effectiveness and cost-benefit-analysis may pay little attention to the effect of decisions on people and their relationships. But the criteria that have to be discovered must be open to the future possibilities for man, and may not define his flourishing simply in terms of a chosen epoch in his past. Such criteria seem bound to involve a hidden theology, some conception of what man is for, of what (to use Lehmann's phrase) 'makes and keeps human life human'.[9] Since this is more accurately a hidden anthropology behind our ethics, it may be possible to hope for a fairly wide agreement. Basil Mitchell has pointed out that the participants in the debate about law, morality and religion all stand within the same civilized Western tradition and share the assumptions about man and society which belong to that tradition. The fact that these assumptions are deeply influenced by the Christian religion is not to the point here. The point is that they are shared by believer and unbeliever alike.

In the rapid change of modern society and the choices that lie before us, there is a need for the definition of common social ends, which claim no universality but are appropriate to a social situation at a period in history – the sort of thing which J. H. Oldham called 'middle axioms'.[10] Such common ends, however, are not axiomatic, but are dependent on common views about man and society. I think it might still be possible to get agreement on such matters – e.g. in relation to social development and planning – among those whose standpoints in religion seem widely separated.

(iii) The middle axioms, common ends, or whatever we care to call them, are always temporary. As the situation changes, so they have to be rethought. In this there is some safeguard against the abuse of moral principles for the maintenance of unjust order. The possibility that in a particular situation one might decide that it is better to take all the risks attendant on the destruction of a social order, than to endure any longer the violence which it does to humanity, cannot be ruled out; but the decision can only be taken realistically if one does not assume that justice will follow automatically on the destruction of a particular form of injustice. The question will remain, what makes the new society human, worthy of man, and what saves it from the rationalizing of its injustices? Here we may borrow an insight from Marx and say that a society is to be judged by the quality of the human relationships that are possible within it. Human life flourishes in human relationships.

Thus while we seek for a modern equivalent to natural law, it is doubtful if the traditional doctrine – the theory – can be rehabilitated. Certainly the doctrine with its view that any human law that is contrary to natural law is not a law but a perversion of law, contains a revolutionary element – a ground for civil disobedience at least; but this aspect has seldom been prominent in its interpretation by the institutions of the law and the church. Certainly also, the doctrine has proved elastic in its application to different situations. If one compares the encyclical *Rerum Novarum* of 1891 with *Populorum Progressio* of 1967 one sees to what different conclusions the doctrine of natural law can lead in its social application. There is indeed a welcome progression from the concern for private property to the concern for social justice. But this elasticity does not inspire confidence in the universality and usefulness of the doctrine of natural law. The fact that the same generalities can be applied in such different ways, from a cautious conservatism to an almost revolutionary urgency, suggests that the generalities are not the important or the decisive things in determining the attitudes. One must also contrast the development of the natural law teaching in the great social encyclicals with the *refusal* to develop it in *Humanae Vitae*, and this in a matter which is vital to the survival of the human race. The time has come for the traditional theory of natural law to be left behind; we must find new ways of exploring and expressing the possibility of a moral consensus among men.

# A Comment from the Roman Catholic Tradition

## ENDA McDONAGH

I am not entirely happy about Woods's summary of the tradition of natural law in the five affirmations given. This is not because they do not present as adequate a summary as other possible affirmations but because they do not open up the problem of natural law to the Christian tradition which has neglected or ignored it, and do not really provide a framework for discussion for people who no longer accept belief in God.

The particular difficulties associated with each of the affirmations are sufficiently discussed by Woods. I should prefer therefore to suggest other approaches to the problem in the hope of meeting the two basic difficulties raised above.

Within the context of Christian ethics the point made by Woods about what is common in different ethical traditions might be applied more exactly to what the Judaeo-Christian tradition shares with and indeed borrows from contemporary secular or at least non-Jewish and non-Christian sources. In particular the decalogue might be examined in its borrowings from Babylonian and other moral traditions. In the New Testament the 'household codes' in the Pauline epistles and the intertwining of the three strands of sayings of the Lord, Old Testament directives and secular morality of the time in Romans 12–14 are two examples of how closely related 'revealed' morality is to non-revealed, that derived from the moral experience of mankind.

A fuller understanding of the Incarnation, together with the theology of the Word in John, and of Christ as the centre of creation as well as of salvation in Paul, would give a sound theological basis for man's own human endowment as the bearer of those moral values through which he may answer the call of the Father and share in the sonship of Jesus.[1]

For theological reasons and in the interests of common understanding it might be better not to use the terms natural or law. The word morality is sufficient and allows for fuller communication.

In speaking to non-Christians and non-believers the appeal can only be through human experience, individual and communal, past and present. This human experience[2] mediates some sense of moral claim which in reflection may lead to some recognition of moral values enshrined in the dignity of man and in practice urges its theoretical opponents in some practical contradiction. This however is open-ended in two senses. It allows for indefinite development in the future, although some criteria of development are necessary. And it admits of opening towards the transcendent at least by raising the question of the ultimate source of this claim, if the experience of the claim and of response to it is not already understood as involving some transcendence of self which cannot be confined within any particular horizon. Along this line of argument the special experience recorded in the Bible and in particular that of Jesus Christ might be seen as interpreting and specifying this more general human experience.

# 5

# The Natural Law and the Law of Christ

## ENDA McDONAGH

In the present task of theological renewal, moral theology is perhaps the section of Catholic theology which is in need of the most sweeping reform. The full extent of that reform or its causes cannot be discussed here. This paper is confined to one central aspect of moral theology as it has been presented in the Catholic tradition, the relation between natural law and revealed morality and the legal expression of both. It will examine this relationship in the light of the basic source of all Christian theology, the revelation of Yahweh which reached its culmination in Jesus Christ, and it will seek to derive some alternative understanding of moral theology, and organization of it, to that given in the manuals and in some versions of renewal.

The title of the paper obviously refers to the constituent elements of the manuals of moral theology as we have known them. They were for the most part composed of natural law commands and prohibitions plus divine positive laws based on revelation (with a generous measure of purely human canon law). The principle of unity was understood in an extrinsic fashion as the will of God, conceived as a law. The far-reaching effects of all this I have discussed elsewhere.[1] Here two points are relevant: the tenuous connection between such moral theology and the revelation made in Christ and the predominant legal form in which morality is conceived and expounded. To evaluate this approach in the elements which compose it and the form in which it is presented, it is necessary to return to revelation as source.

I

In studying the Judaeo-Christian revelation as source of morality, the theologian discovers that what is of first importance is not the explicit moral directives contained therein but the framework in which they are set, the very structure of revelation itself. This structure emerges clearly in the Old and New Testament revelations and may be described as a covenant (*berith, diatheke, testamentum*) structure in accordance with the predominant description of the revelation. In this structure God reveals himself by entering into relationship with Israel (mankind), whereby Israel belongs to him in a special way, enjoys his special favour but must respond to this divine initiative in its way of life. God's self-revelation is in fact a self-giving which demands a human response, which is also a self-giving. Moral theology studies the human response demanded in the light of the divine self-giving. Divine revelation is seen as invitation demanding response, as gift and task (*donum et mandatum, Gabe und Aufgabe*), as announcement of God's favour or salvation and instruction about the realization of that favour in one's life (*kerygma* and *didache*). And while all this is verified of the various stages of the Old Testament revelation to the first Israel, it emerges in its full force in the New Testament or covenant achieved in the person, life, death and glorification of Jesus Christ, founder of the new Israel.[2] It is only in this context and with this structure that it is possible to have a Christian moral theology at all.

The task of moral theology then is not to study the 'law of God' but that divine self-giving we call revelation as a way of life for man. In the central exchange between God and man in the Old Testament revelation, the Mosaic covenant, the law, for all its legal form appears as the way of *response* appropriate to God's people in consequence of his choice of them. It is this choice and the activity in which it has been so clearly expressed which is the basis of the obligations of the people, and the source of their capacity to fulfil them. When this gift-aspect of the covenant and response which it demands is forgotten, and the material demands are treated as a way of establishing in human fashion a claim against God, the Mosaic law becomes, in the Pauline image, sin instead of grace or gift.[3]

This distortion of his gifts did not prevent God from completing his planned self-giving by sending his own Son. With the event of

Jesus Christ, the self-revealing and self-giving of God to man reaches its ultimate point. God himself became man. In Jesus Christ the relationship between God and man attained its fullest depth by sharing the divine sonship, and its widest range as offered to all men. In him the divine gift and the human response reached their climax. Through him and only through him, God the Father comes to man and man comes to the Father. As a study of the way of life manifest in the New Covenant, moral theology is centred on Christ. He is the Way. The human activity appropriate to man in his life, or in any individual situation of it, must be a response of one called to be a son of the Father after the manner and by the power of Christ. Jesus Christ constitutes in his totality the norm or standard of good activity in the present order. He is, if we wish to use the expression, the moral law.

This could be developed in more systematic fashion by analysing the teaching of Eph. 1.9–10; Col. 1.15–20, the Logos doctrine of St John, and the New Testament preoccupation with Christ as the one mediator between God and man. He is the centre not only of redemption but also of creation.

It could be traced in more elementary fashion in his call and instruction of his disciples. They were not just called to learn from him as from other rabbis. They must share his attitudes and imitate his actions. Eventually they must share his life and destiny in a way that had no human parallels. It was an internal, transforming share as branches of the vine or organs of the human body. The life which should issue in their activity was, in Paul's insistent phrase, life in Christ. And this could be expressed in terms of some participation in the divine being. Through the gift of the Spirit they had become brothers and coheirs with Christ as sons of the Father. In their lives as a whole and in each individual moral situation, they were faced with an invitation from the Father to which they might only respond as sons.

The being which must now decide their moral activity (according to the axiom, *actio sequitur esse*) was the being of the incarnate Son of God which they had been called to share (*esse filii incarnati*). Without wishing to deny the necessity of describing moral realities in such ontological terms, it is well to be aware of the dangers involved, e.g. of misunderstanding our own terms and restricting *esse* in such a way that it regards history as an external and acci- dental category or reality, or extending the being too far to include, for example, biological elements in an undifferentiated way.[4] And for many people outside the scholastic metaphysical tradition, the axiom makes no moral sense whatever. In discussing the further characteristics of the morality revealed in Christ, this axiom will not therefore be much in evidence.

Given this underlying structure of God's self-giving in Christ demanding human response in Christ, Christian morality might be explored and expounded in various ways. For our purposes it will be sufficient to draw attention to some characteristic aspects of it, which have to be taken into account, whatever particular way or model is used.

The most obvious of these has already been stressed – its character as gift or grace. It is solely the initiative of God which is responsible for this covenanted relationship. It is his gift of himself in Christ which calls for man's response and enables man to make it. Every moral response will have a thanksgiving or eucharistic character. Any presentation of morality which contradicts or obscures this basic gift character by setting up or appearing to set up a human claims system is so far unchristian.

In the context in which it is given the gift is a reconciling gift. It restores sinful man to divine favour. The call to response becomes a call to repentance. Man's self-giving to God must take the form of return, *shub*, *metanoia*. His life-task as well as each individual action will have a penitential element, as he seeks more fully to be freed from entanglements of the sin of the world and of his own personal sin.[5] In responding to the Father in Christ he will find it necessary to die to self in its egoistic desires. He must be crucified with Christ to share the new life and new creation of his resurrection, to share his sonship. God's total gift of self demands man's total gift in return, and that can be achieved only if one is willing to take up the cross and follow Christ. The cross is an inescapable element in the good life of the Christian, in Christian morality.

The reconciling gift establishes man in a special relationship with the Father and with his fellow-man. As son of the Father he is brother of his fellow-man and *vice versa*. His moral task is the living or expression of these relationships, which are really different aspects of the one relationship. So Christ could sum up the Christian life as love of God and love of neighbour, where that means all mankind, including one's enemies. St John pinpoints love of neighbour as test of one's love of God, and St Paul reduces all commandments to love of neighbour. This is not the New Testament's way of emphasizing the primacy of love among equals or as one commandment among others.[6] The new commandment of Jesus derives from the new relationship(s) revealed in him. It is the primary articulation of the demands of that relationship. All other moral demands are particular expressions of love as sonship or brotherhood.

The relational/love character of Christian morality must not be understood in any narrow I-Thou, personalist terms. In Christ each man is related to all others. This will achieve an immediately personal expression (in varying degrees) with only a limited number of people. With most people it can be expressed only through different social institutions. The full *community* range of Christian morality can be understood in the context of God's self-giving to mankind. This has always been directed to a people or community. It has been understood only in community. And its purpose has been the establishment of community.[7] The community to be established emerges in the New Testament as the community of all mankind without any distinction of Jew or Gentile, bond or free. The working for the establishment of such a community at the individual and institutional level is clearly implied in the relationship one enjoys in Christ.

The very brief reference to the community dimension of Christian morality, possible here, leads naturally into its related historical dimension. God's self-giving to man-in-community has a history and so necessarily has man's response. It was only in and through the course of human history that the God-man relationship (like any human relationship) could be achieved. Although complicated by man's sin, his historical infidelity, the relationship did progress to the point of Jesus Christ and an explicit sharing of the divine sonship with man. And the completion of that sharing lies in the future. It is still promise and hope.

At the centre of this historical development stands Jesus Christ. As future Messiah, present Redeemer, and the Lord who is to come, he is the underlying meaning of every stage of that relationship. So he can now be seen to constitute, in varying degrees of realization and understanding, the way for all men at all times to the Father, their standard of behaviour as sons. When the God-man relationship realized in him is understood to include the total man in all his created reality, and Jesus is seen to incorporate this, it is easier to grasp how all men at all times, whatever their explicit relation to formal salvation history, have been included in the scope of that history and been related to Christ as its centre and Lord. This is not intended to obscure the importance of the explicit relationship, without which we could not speak in these terms at all. Nor is it intended to minimize the very real differences in moral understanding which have always existed and still exist, or to suggest that such moral differences cannot sometimes, perhaps frequently, be justified. On the contrary we must accept such historical and cultural differences as are due not just to human sinfulness (some are), but as part of the historical character of man, part of his divine endowment in fact, and as confirmed and given ultimate meaning in the historical relationship between God and man, which is revealed in Christ.

For the community, historical development in the moral tasks demanded by the relationship to God and to one another and in the understanding of these tasks is indisputable. But this development is no less true of the individual person. It has found expression in the recognition of growth in moral understanding and responsibility, through which each person has to pass. It might be extended to a recognition that every moral action is a response from a particular personal and cultural situation and that it is a good response, the response of a son and brother, if it expresses movement towards the Father as he expresses himself in this particular situation, if it expresses growth and development rather than if it stays on one side of a certain line or fulfils a particular legal demand. In spatial terms moral action is not staying in one place (in the 'state of grace'), it is going somewhere (towards the Father and the brother). Moral theology and pastoral practice need to take the historical character of the individual moral life much more seriously.

The historical dimension of Christian morality, at the community and personal levels, may not then be taken as meaning simply that this morality has a past, that it has gone through certain stages of development to reach the present definitive stage. In fact it is no less orientated towards the future now than at previous stages of development. The Old Testament promise was fulfilled in the New by the revelation of a better promise and of the way to receive it. The redemption accomplished in Jesus is an earnest of the future available to all men in him. Their path to that future lies in history, in the succession of presents that leads out of the past into the future. The Christian task involves using resources inherited from the past to transform the present and to bring closer the final, eschatological fulfilment. Christian morality has an eschatological character. It is preparing the future.[8]

The preparation is in virtue of a gift and it is for a gift. It may not be interpreted as a purely human task or achievement, or approached as if a realization of the final kingdom in this world by man were possible. On the other hand we may not evade this task on the plea of leaving it to God. We may not retreat into a private area of life as the area of moral activity and refuse to take part in the transformation of the world as service to our brother and our Father. Man's response to the Father's self-giving must in its totality involve entrusting himself completely to the God of the future, to God as he emerges in the unknown and uncontrollable future into which man has to move. For the individual's final decisive step into that absolute future (which is God), the step he takes at dying, each important moral action in his life should have prepared him as a trusting step into the unknown towards God and his fellow-man. This moral activity has as its other dimension a step into the unknown for the community also, but this will be more evident in some decisions and in some people's lives than in others. Yet it may never be entirely absent from any. Personal eschatological fulfilment is to be achieved in and through the community. Any step towards the one fulfilment is a step, however limited, towards the other.

Given the dominating role of Christ in this outline of Christian morality and the age-old tradition of describing morality in terms of law, it is to be expected that the Pauline phrase 'the law of Christ' would be invoked here.[9] St Thomas Aquinas seems concerned with the same reality when he speaks of the *lex nova*.[10] And the tradition which presents morality as a law has obvious and good reason in the obligatory character of moral demands. Yet from what has been already said of the origin and character of Christian morality, the word 'law' cannot be used here in the same sense in which it is used of human law.

St Thomas makes this clear when he points out that the *lex nova* is primarily an unwritten law, a law stamped on our being (*lex indita*) by the presence of the Holy Spirit[11] 'whereby we cry Abba, Father'.[12] It is a law internal to us, the shape of our divine sonship as it seeks expression in our daily lives with all the characteristics which we have already seen. It is not a law imposed on us from the outside as a human law might be. And it is not a detailed code of written law to be found in the scripture. There is a written or formulated aspect to it. Otherwise it could not be the object of our discussion at all. This written or formulated aspect does not refer primarily to particular commands but to the reality of the gift, relationship, etc., which we have to live. However it is possible and necessary to go further, after the example of Jesus and the apostolic writers, and to formulate commands, ranging from the all-embracing command of charity to much more particular ones such as the prohibition of lying. The more particular such commands become, the more restricted their field of application. It is impossible to prescribe for the living of a relationship, which is what Christian morality is about, by a detailed code. To attempt to do so destroys the relationship, as later Judaism discovered. Such formulated demands as are necessary should be kept to a minimum, presented as secondary and derived, although necessary to the living relationship which they attempt to express. And the creative character of the relationship, by which new and developing responses are recognized and sought out, should never be obscured, as it is in the usual legal presentation of morality.

Legal formulations such as are found in the Old and New Testament are secondary, derivative and approximate. A formulation of very general application cannot give very precise directions for the individual case and the very precise formulation cannot apply to very many situations. The personal creative character of the relationship involved, in which each man has his own vocation, does not allow for more than a recognition of the general structures common to all such relationships (as revealed in Christ), structures which must be realized in each good response.

The formulation of these is necessary to deliberate Christian living and they may take legal form as commandments or prohibitions. In addition the moral wisdom and experience of the community and of the individual will offer guidelines for normal Christian living which may not be arbitrarily ignored. But the more exact understanding of the general structures, and so the more exact formulation of commands and prohibitions based on them, is a continuing task of the (Christian) community. So for example the respect for the life of the neighbour, which emerges from the structure of brotherhood, has gone through various stages of refinement in regard to self-defence, capital punishment and war. And development is far from complete in each case. More remote guidelines, such as those in regard to property, are more provisional still. It is when one begins with the legal formulation as the primary moral reality that many of the confusions and dilemmas of moral debate arise. For the Christian theologian the legal form should never be the starting-point.

One might summarize at this stage by saying: Christian morality, the way of life revealed in Christ, is distinguished primarily by its structure in Christ. It is based on the reconciling gift of sonship whereby all men are called to turn from their self-centred behaviour and to behave as sons of the Father and brothers of one another. It is personal to each man, yet to each man as member of the (human) community. It is universal in its range, but realized in different historical forms. It emerges from God's historic interventions in the past, but deals with the present as it prepares for the eschatological completion of the divine activity and the God-man relationship. It urges or obliges at the very core of man's existence and so may be described in an analogous way as a law. Its demands need to be formulated, if it is to be lived as response. But these formulations are limited in value and approximate in meaning. Detailed legal prescriptions must always be judged in the light of the basic relationship and may never be substituted for it.

## II

All this offers a very different picture from the conventional manual of moral theology. In particular, where does the treatment of natural law which played such a large role in the manual fit in? The rest of this paper will be devoted to the attempt to answer this question.

It may be easier to begin by excluding one commonly accepted view of the place of natural law in Christian morality. This view, with its two-storey image of the relation between nature and grace, regards Christian morality as composed of the simple addition of natural law (applicable to all men) and divine positive law (applicable to Christians). In the only existing order, in which all men are called to be sons of the Father in Christ, no such simple separation and addition is possible. It presupposes some natural order separate from the order of grace (and refusal of grace), which can be isolated and studied as such. And it usually understands both natural and divine positive law as capable of adequate, if not complete, expression in legal commands and prohibitions. They can then be more easily added together. But all men exist within the one order subject to, modified by, reconciled by and finally judged by, the divine self-giving in Christ. This is the structure of the situation within which they must make their moral decisions and perform their moral actions however far they are aware or unaware of this structure. There is no purely natural order which may be the subject of moral experience and reflection on that experience.

A quite different view emerges if one begins from the single reality which is there – man called to be son and brother in Christ. The key-figure is, of course, the God-man. But the point of the Incarnation was not somehow to distort or diminish man in his humanity, but rather to affirm and confirm his worth and dignity. In becoming man God paid his full respect, as it were, to man's humanity. Theology today is rightly insisting on the genuineness and completeness of this humanity of Jesus. According to the model and by the power of the Incarnation, each of us can become truly a son of the Father and brother of one another in and through our human endowment.

As it is possible to distinguish reflexively between the human and divine in Jesus Christ (although they were inseparable in reality), it is also possible (and necessary) to distinguish in men called to be sons of God and so modified in their existence, between the human and the divine (or its modifying effect). The (moral) response, which men must make to this call in their whole lives or in any particular situation, can in its inseparable unity be distinguished at the reflexive level in this conceptual way.[13] It is, if it is a good response, truly and completely the act of a son of the Father and so the expression of this gift of sonship, and at the same time truly and fully a human act. Indeed in the light of the Incarnation it can only be the act of a son (and brother) in so far as it is a fully human act, and (again however unconsciously) a truly human act if it is an act of a son (and brother). The way to sonship and brotherhood in Christ is in and through the human; and fulness of humanity, attainable in history in degrees, must await eschatological completion as sons and brothers.

In so far as the natural law derives from man's human nature as the moral activity appropriate to or demanded by that human nature, it can be found and distinguished within the present order to the extent that human nature can. There are, however, many conceptual difficulties involved here. Human nature, as it is experienced, is that modified by the divine call and its history as we have seen. Secondly human nature does not appear except in a certain cultural, historical form which is subject to deep change, so that it is very difficult to isolate with concrete human nature those features which, as constituting it or pertaining to it at the metaphysical level, might provide a basis for morality, according to the axiom, *actio sequitur esse*.[14] As a result of this difficulty, particular historical realizations have been accepted as part of the metaphysical essence of man or, even worse, particular sub-philosophical categories (e.g. biological) have been confused with it. Finally there is considerable dispute among Catholic natural law theorists about how it should be conceived, grounded and formulated, while, of course it is not for the most part acceptable to Christian moralists outside the Catholic tradition.

In spite of all these very real difficulties a place can be found for natural law in a renewed Catholic version of Christian morality.[15] And this is true, whichever of the two more coherent and influential conceptions of natural law is favoured: that which identifies nature as the human capacity of recognizing man's inescapable moral condition – that he is called to do the good and avoid evil (Aquinas), or that which concentrates on man's metaphysical nature as the basis for good human behaviour (late scholasticism and most subsequent Catholic thinking).[16] That man has such a capacity is presupposed in the God-man dialogue and necessarily persists in it. That he has a metaphysical human nature distinct from the divine and preserved in its humanity is equally presupposed in the dialogue. Without these two realities the dialogue would not be possible at all. In that context the Incarnation provides a guarantee for the reality and integrity of man's humanity, its capacity for moral knowledge and the moral possibilities inherent in it. These may be realized in widely differing ways in the course of history but they can never contradict certain basic directions, without diminishing or destroying that humanity. What these directions are is very difficult to formulate in a way that will not involve some historical conditioning of man. Yet this does not rule out the value of doing so or invalidate the notion of a natural law conceived in this way. Briefly then it may be said that natural law, as the absolute if general obligation to behave morally of which man (as man) is aware or the general moral possibilities and obligations which derive from his (metaphysical) human nature, is contained and affirmed within the order of incarnation and redemption. Natural law does not exist outside or apart from this order.

As the Son of God became man Jesus Christ constitutes the centre of the moral order, incorporating in himself the moral possibilities enshrined in humanity, which taken in abstraction may be described as the natural law. Where, in accordance with the Logos theology of St John and the Pauline theology of Colossians and Ephesians, he is seen as the centre of creation as well as of redemption, the foundation of natural law morality in him appears in a deeper and fuller light.

Natural law then has its place in a morality centred on Christ. There remain certain difficulties about the very term which call for brief discussion. The word 'natural' as used here may be very misleading for people who normally employ it, in association with law, for the laws of nature, the physical, chemical, biological and other laws. Indeed some of this confusion has affected theologians themselves as the recent contraception debate made clear. Taken in the technical, theological, sense as opposed to 'supernatural', it almost inevitably leads to thinking in terms of a two-storey morality as mentioned earlier. The word 'law', if in association with 'natural' it escapes being thought of in the sense of physical law and is taken as moral law, is in grave danger of being assimilated to the notion of 'positive law', imposed on man by an external lawgiver and in an extrinsic way. It would become a collection of commands and prohibitions which would in practice be treated as on the same level with human and positive commands and prohibitions. There are too many examples of this in recent moral teaching and practice for the danger to be ignored. And of course such a concept of natural law is quite foreign to the thinking of Aquinas and the best in the natural law tradition. It might be in the interest of that tradition and of the reality which it calls natural law to drop the term altogether.

What matters is that we recognize man's capacity for and awareness of morality, and the respect which this involves for the basic structure of his being as man, and affirm that all this has been preserved, deepened and – it may be said – ultimately founded in the Incarnation. For the moral demands which arise in human experience without reference to the underlying Christian structure – and this occurs for all men much of the time and for the majority (non-Christians) all of the time – it would suffice to speak of 'morality', the moral order, moral obligation or moral values. The qualifications 'natural' or 'Christian' may be misleading or unacceptable and clarify nothing for the problem at issue. Within the Christian community, in an effort to understand the moral order fully, its foundation in Christ and the consequent characteristics, already discussed, will have an important role. In dialogue with others the foundation and characteristics will always be implicit. They may have to become explicit to demonstrate that we are being faithful to our own basic understanding, not betraying it or cheating by pretending that something accepted in secular morality can be reconciled with, even deepened by, Christianity.

Reflection on the moral order in which we live is a necessary human task. Christians believe that this reflection is carried on in the order of grace or God's gift of himself to mankind. So the reflecting subject (person in community) and the object reflected upon (humanity in person and community) are under the enlightening and transforming power of the divine gift. This need not be consciously adverted to in many instances. Sometimes conscious attention to the divine dimension may obscure the human, prevent it from being given its full value, or by the use of religious terms hinder exact moral analysis. Christians also suffer the consequences of the sin of the world. Non-Christians also enjoy the enlightening power of the Spirit and in some situations, free from such temptations, they may arrive more quickly and surely at a correct moral understanding. Christians must always be aware of their particular temptations and be ready to learn from all. Moral theologians must be ready to accept and integrate the valid moral insights of all men, and thereby try to outline a scheme of morality which does justice to all the elements of that order in which man is called to achieve the fulness of his humanity as son of the Father and brother of all other men.

Within this structure of morality, centred on Christ, the moral values enshrined in created humanity and discovered in the history of human reflection find their true place. It is misleading, however, to describe them as natural or to conceive them as primarily legal in form. The traditional notion of the natural law persists in a genuine way in such an approach to moral theology, but in an important sense it is neither natural nor a law.

# 6

# The Bible and Christian Ethics

## BARNABAS LINDARS, SSF

### I

The purpose of this essay is to try to determine in what sense the Bible can be used as a basis of Christian ethics. The fact that this is questionable arises from changes in our attitudes to both. Modern developments of biblical criticism have tended to undermine the moral authority of the Bible. At the same time moral discourse has moved into areas where the Bible gives little or no direct guidance. Moreover in our contemporary society there is a marked tendency to reject authoritarianism in morals. The Ten Commandments appear to belong to a long-faced religion which is now dead. It is, in fact, precisely as an authority that the Bible has chiefly been valued for the purposes of ethics. In spite of its vast size it does not contain many moral laws or practical rules which apply to most people's lives. But it does contain *some*, and these have had all the weight of the privileged position of an accepted sacred book to give them authority. It is doubtful whether the Bible is now capable of exercising such an authority, even if people wanted it. It will be necessary first to say something about the reasons for the very different valuation of the Bible which results from modern study, before attempting to make some constructive suggestions for the future. We may first consider the Bible as a direct guide to moral living, that is to say, as a book of rules under divine sanctions. In spite of what has just been said, the collections of rules of one kind or another are quite sizable. There are the laws in the Pentateuch, many of them, it is true, concerned with the minutiae of sacrificial worship, but also covering the norms of family life and agrarian society. There are also the moral precepts of the book of Proverbs and other products of the Wisdom schools. In the historical books and particularly in the prophets there is a deep moral concern from which moral guidance may be obtained. In the New Testament the gospels have considerable moral content in the teaching of Jesus, and the epistles frequently contain direct moral precepts. From the point of view of the history of the canon of scripture, the Pentateuch, as the law, or Torah, first gained canonical status specifically as a code of laws to be observed by the Jewish people who held it sacred. Its deficiencies as a guide to the whole of life were made good by the rabbinic casuistry, resulting in a mass of rulings known as the Halakah. Although the books of the New Testament cannot be compared with the Torah, the fixing of the canon tended to have the same effect. It is well known that the lists of duties in the epistles (the 'household codes') follow pagan models, but their content is closely related to the central teaching of the gospel, so that they could easily form the basis of a Christian moral code. This also has been the subject of casuistry in the hands of Christian moralists.

If Christian ethics is the art of distinguishing right from wrong in the business of Christian living, then the Bible, as the deposit of the fundamental documents of the Christian revelation, may be expected to provide the primary clues for this art. The attitude towards the Torah as a book of rules was extended by the Jews themselves to the whole of the Old Testament. Christians naturally give pride of place to the New Testament, but the Old has continued to be valued for its ethical content. Thus the Bible as a whole has been regarded as a book of moral laws. Historically speaking, the Bible has never been in practice the sole source of moral laws. In the western tradition, at any rate, there has been a vast infusion of laws from Roman jurisprudence. In the Roman Church the sacrosanct character of the biblical laws has been extended to papal pronouncements and the *magisterium* of the church. The Reformation, however, tended to transfer this authority to the Bible alone. At least this was what was claimed, even though moral traditions were largely prefabricated, and really only employed the Bible as the authoritative sanction for them.

There is here the basis for the common rather naïve idea that the Bible can and should supply all the answers to moral questions. If I am asked why I observe a particular rule, I can answer that it is because the Bible says so. From this point of view the Bible tends to be regarded as the inspired Word of God. It is virtually the *vox Dei*.

With such an attitude the distinction between the two Testaments is largely ignored, or at best seriously misunderstood. The attitude to the Bible is uncritical, and easily lapses into superstition. But it is worth pondering this approach a little, because it gives rise to certain exegetical questions. These remain operative to some extent, even when the presuppositions of this approach are seen to be invalid and are accordingly abandoned.

The questions that arise are of two kinds. First there are questions of interpretation, what one may call pure exegesis. If appeal is made to a particular text, it must be asked whether the words really mean what they appear to mean. Is the translation correct? Is it made from a secure text, or is there reason to suspect textual corruption? There may be error at either of these points, but the mistake may go further back, being inherent in the sacred text itself. The tenth commandment is an example of this. Ex. 20.17 reads (*RSV*): 'You shall not covet your neighbour's house; you shall not covet your neighbour's wife . . .', whereas Deut. 5.21 has: 'Neither shall you covet your neighbour's wife; and you shall not desire your neighbour's house. . . .' It is now recognized that the word translated 'covet' changed its meaning in the course of time, and that this is why the two versions differ. Originally it meant 'misappropriate', and was only later confined to the thought that lies behind the action. This has been made explicit in the Deuteronomic version, which uses a different word in the parallel clause. Moreover the wife has been mentioned before the house, because, from the point of view of motive, lust is more serious than avarice. If the tenth commandment is regarded as God speaking, we are entitled to ask what he is really demanding of the conscience of man. Is it the identifiable offence of stealing which is forbidden, or is it the inner desire, which may well be involuntary at its first onset? There are other questions which also have to be faced, and already appear in this example. What is the actual scope of reference of the command? Is it confined to a particular set of historical conditions, or does it apply universally? What are the criteria for deciding how to apply it to oneself, assuming that it is taken to be the divine command to all men?

The second kind of question is also illustrated in the above example. The two different forms, once their real distinction has been discovered, pose the problem of contradictions. How can they be reconciled? Is one authoritative and not the other? It need hardly be pointed out that the *vox Dei* approach is unwilling to admit that real contradictions exist. Then much ingenuity has to be expended in reconciling the irreconcilable. The results are not likely to be very convincing. Similar ingenuity is required to make commands applicable when they really refer to what is obsolete. The Christian use of Leviticus is the obvious example here. If it still contains a message for Christians, the numerous ceremonial laws will have to undergo a considerable reinterpretation. From the days of Philo onwards this has been done by allegorical exegesis, by which the practical details are made to refer to moral dispositions. This tends to impose a non-biblical ethics upon the Bible, and so contradicts the pure exegesis. It has to be recognized that there are varieties of ethical thought in the Bible, that it is not always self-consistent, and that much of the Old Testament is obsolete and inapplicable to later ages. The *vox Dei* approach to the Bible cannot be maintained because of the nature of the Bible itself. There is, however, a reduced form of this approach which may still be considered valid, and to this we now turn.

## II

Our second approach takes as its starting-point the manifest distinction between the Old Testament and the New. This is more promising, because the distinction is recognized within the New Testament itself. We may think of the series of contrasts in the Sermon on the Mount between what was 'said by the men of old' and the new precepts of Jesus himself. Here surely is a basis for a genuinely Christian ethics, untroubled by the difficulties just mentioned. The same exegetical questions must be asked, of course, but there is a better prospect of reaching satisfactory results. So we begin by saying that the Old Testament is superseded by Christ. He alone provides all that is needed for Christian ethics. But does this mean that the Old Testament can be simply written off? We almost have this situation today, when most Christians have some knowledge of the gospels, but little if any of the Old Testament. This is by no means a new situation, for St Paul's Gentile converts were in a somewhat similar position. But it is one thing to say as a matter of theology that the law is superseded in Christ, quite another to make this the basis of ethics. This was a matter of vital concern to St Paul. In his epistles we can see an unresolved tension between the need to deny the validity of certain essential parts of the Jewish law (circumcision is the big issue) and the equally pressing necessity of retaining many of the fundamental ethical positions of the Old Testament against antinomian tendencies.

It thus becomes necessary to modify the original statement and to say that Christ confirms the fundamentals of the law, but also supersedes it. The words of Christ become the basis for deducing the norms of Christian behaviour, interpreted both by his personal example and by the teaching of the epistles. Some use, too, must be made of the Old Testament, but only in so far as it is consonant with the teaching of Christ, and in fact is presupposed by it. Thus the ten commandments have their reaffirmation in Christ, though modified by his preference for the summary of the law given in Mark 12.28–31. With these important qualifications it can be claimed that the teaching of Jesus gives an authoritative basis of Christian ethics. The position is similar to the last one, if it is expected that his teaching will serve as a book of rules under divine sanctions. His words are treated as the *vox Dei*, instead of the whole Bible. And the attitude remains legalistic, as the words of Christ are taken as ethical prescriptions in just the same way as the commands of the Old Testament, even though this is superseded except in so far as his teaching confirms it.

It is probably true to say that this is the attitude of the average Christian today. He cannot cope with the Old Testament, but he does expect the gospels at least to give him direct guidance in the task of Christian living. But it is probably also true that the average Christian takes this line with a heavy heart. For he soon discovers that many of Christ's demands are 'impossible'. Turning the other cheek is bad enough. Loving one's enemies – really loving them – is excessively difficult. Making up one's quarrels before nightfall, even within weeks or months, is often impracticable, especially as it takes two to make up a quarrel. Seeing Christ in one's neighbour, and giving to everyone who asks, impose too great a burden. Even the most serious Christian soon finds that he has to content himself with an uneasy compromise which is far from being ethically satisfactory.

## III

The teaching of Christ fails to work when simply taken as a divinely sanctioned book of rules. So it becomes necessary to attempt another, more sophisticated, approach. This consists in trying to find the principles that lie behind Christ's teaching in order to have a basis for moral decisions which will be distinctively Christian. This involves serious biblical exegesis, and will include the exegetical questions which have already been referred to. The demands of Christ have to be collected with due attention to problems of text and translation and to their context in the circumstances of his life and ministry. Then they have to be classified and assessed. By this means it is hoped that the 'impossible' demands may be brought under an inclusive principle which can accommodate them in a way that is satisfying to the Christian conscience. A short cut may be taken by noting what appears to be most fundamental in the teaching of Jesus, and seeing how the particular demands fit into it. Here the fourth gospel comes to our aid by the extreme simplicity of its ethical content. Jesus says repeatedly that he does the will of God. This is not a satisfactory basis by itself, however, because we need some principle in order to discover what is the will of God. The Johannine literature (epistles as well as gospel) emphasize the command to 'love one another'. This gives *agape* as the basic principle. It can now be said that the life and teaching of Jesus are the divinely given expression of *agape*.

The advantage of this approach is that the moral authority of Jesus is not only maintained, but appears to be positively enhanced. His words are listened to with the greatest respect. The harsh demands are governed by the principle of *agape*, and so one can dare to take them seriously. In fact this principle provides an escape route at the same time. For obviously they cannot be applied in all circumstances. *Agape* itself suggests that other factors may have to be taken into consideration, so that in a given instance it will be more loving to do the exact opposite (e.g. to refuse to respond to the request of an alcoholic). The recognition of wider factors makes it possible to avoid the moral obligation to a slavishly literal following of the gospel precepts without any lessening of their intrinsic value. Moreover the way is opened to extend the range of moral application, so as to cover the numerous facets of life which are not specifically mentioned in the New Testament. So the task of Christian ethics today is often conceived as an exploration of the meaning of *agape*, taken as the fundamental principle of the ethics of Jesus.

Nevertheless, for all its attractiveness, this view is open to a number of objections. It is probably no accident that it has come to the fore at a time when there is strong pressure to cast off the restraints of fixed rules and ethical norms. It actually reduces the moral authority of Christ when it is used as a pretext to set his commands aside. It still rests upon the presupposition that Jesus has a moral authority for today, which is by no means axiomatic, as we shall see in a moment. It is also doubtful whether it is possible to bring all moral questions under this one heading, especially as the word 'love', even when all erotic connotations are carefully excluded, still retains emotional content.

## IV

Our last section has been concerned with what may be termed the 'agapeistic' view of New Testament ethics. It was suggested that this is reached by means of a short cut, rather than by careful exegesis of the teaching of Jesus. When we address ourselves to this task, we find that it raises serious difficulties in the way of discovering a basis for Christian ethics. It cannot be simply taken for granted that the command to love one another is the essential moral message of Christ. In fact it sounds suspiciously like the effect of the older Liberal Protestant picture of Jesus, which was shattered over sixty years ago by Albert Schweitzer's *Quest of the Historical Jesus*.[1] Biblical criticism has to face not only the question of what Jesus actually said, but also the issues that govern the interpretation of what he said: *who* he was, and what was he really trying to do.

There are, then, three questions to answer before the *agape* approach can be accepted, and the first is the question of authenticity. So much of the gospels has been removed by the critical scalpel that it is hard to recover exactly what it was that Jesus said. No critic, of course, denies that there is a substantial deposit of authentic material in the gospels, but there is scarcely a verse which does not show some sign of reshaping in the light of changing needs of the church during the oral stage of transmission. It is hardly possible for the untrained reader to know what he should accept and what he should reject. In any case it is widely known that the words of Jesus in the fourth gospel are on a different footing from the synoptic tradition, so that even the command of *agape* cannot be taken simply and directly as *ipsissima verba* of Jesus. The result is a vague and general feeling that the gospel tradition has been discredited, and that we cannot hope to discover what Jesus really said about anything for certain. The fact that experts disagree ought to prevent people from jumping to radical conclusions, but on the whole it gives cold comfort.

The second question is that of christology. Can the idea of Jesus as the perfect moral teacher stand up to the critical assessment of him? The presuppositions of the critical method positively necessitate some measure of detachment from traditional Christian dogma on the part of the critic. The picture of Jesus which emerges from the critic's researches is not encouraging to those who want to hear in his words the voice of God speaking to them directly. It is far too like the deluded revolutionary of Schweitzer's *Quest*. In fact a great deal of constructive work has been done since then, but it will be more appropriately considered under our third question. For the moment it is enough to mention the critical presupposition, that Jesus is to be seen from the point of view of the Jewish setting of the first century, rather than *sub specie aeternitatis*, and that this setting tends to emphasize his humanity and his Jewishness. This has very much influenced the popular estimate of him. The discovery of the Dead Sea Scrolls, the Israeli excavations of Masada, and recent work on the Zealots, have thrown into relief the political aspects. It is a more masculine picture than that of the liberal school. There is an idealism in it which appeals to youth. He appears as a kind of Ché Guevara. His words are worth paying attention to, but can lay no claim to absolute authority.

This popular feeling has its counterpart in the real difficulties which face theologians in their attempt to construct a christology without God. From this point of view Gethsemane rather than the resurrection is the most illuminating source of guidance for deciding 'What think ye of Christ?' It is an existential approach, for which all talk of moral absolutes is anathema. It means that the sayings of Jesus have to be taken as 'insights', perhaps very illuminating insights, which may be set against other observations, but have no *a priori* force as moral sanctions, apart from their own intrinsic worth. They are not to be taken as rules, creating a binding obligation, but rather as suggestions, or guiding lines, which men may profitably use in seeking to tackle moral problems. But this negative result is not wholly unfortunate. It is arguable that it comes close to the real meaning of the gospel of love, that it sets the 'impossible' demand in a realistic context, and that it makes a suitably flexible basis for the complexity of ethical questions. In other words, it is easily brought into the scope of 'situation ethics', in which the essential *agape* of the Christian revelation remains true to itself, without being warped into the legalism which is fundamentally opposed to it. In both cases, the popular estimate, and the serious

theological endeavour, we can see the influence of the current debate
on christology, with its emphasis on the humanity of Jesus, the one
tending to social idealism, the other to existentialism, but both
reducing the status of Jesus as moral authority.

So now we must look at the effect of recent study on the estimate
of what Jesus was trying to do, or rather of what was achieved in
him. It is universally accepted today that his work was concerned
with the coming kingdom, or rule, of God, and that he conceived of
his own destiny as bound up with it in some sense. Schweitzer's
emphasis on the eschatological and apocalyptic elements in his
teaching is reaffirmed. But instead of seeing this as a misguided
delusion, modern study takes this with the utmost seriousness. The
proclamation of the kingdom is taken in close connection with the
healing miracles and other recorded episodes of the life of Jesus. The
result is a credible picture of Jesus, which does justice to the Jewish
background, but also allows for his distinctiveness, and does not
entail any diminution of his greatness as a moral teacher. But at the
same time it forces a fresh look at the ethical teaching, which now
has to be interpreted in the light of the total message and work of
Jesus. His moral sayings can no longer be pulled out of context and
treated as timeless ethical norms. The treatment of the parables is
the classic example of this change of approach. Formerly they were
held to be moral allegories, from which an unchanging moral truth
could be extracted by stripping off the pictorial details. Now they
are seen to be extremely closely related to the work of preparing
men for the coming kingdom, applicable in the first instance only to
those who actually listened to them and had to form their minds for
an event which was expected in the near future. The fresh applications which they have received, and which have greatly affected their
form in the course of transmission even in the pre-literary stage, are
regarded as invalid. It must be confessed that it is often easier to
perceive the meaning of the subsequent layers than of the original
parable.

The proclamation of the coming kingdom may not seem at first
sight to have any special relevance for ethics. But the uniqueness of
Jesus' teaching on the kingdom is his extreme awareness of the
ethical issues involved. It is a message of mercy in so far as the
action of God to restore the fortunes of his people is itself a sign that
former sins are forgiven and God and man are reconciled. Jesus
shows that such mercy cannot be presumed on, but creates funda-

mental moral obligations. By the same token it is a message of judgment, if these obligations are not heeded. The sense of crisis and immediacy is so strong, that it has been doubted whether his teaching is concerned at all with the time that follows the inaugura-tion of the kingdom. It is now recognized, however, that the ethical sayings do give expression to moral attitudes which are not only required before God's act of salvation, but also continue to be applicable, and therefore become universal, after it has taken place. In so far as this act of salvation was actually achieved in Christ, a further aspect enters into the time scale. The kingdom is present in his person, but its full extent is yet to be reached. It is for this reason that both Paul and John substitute the idea of being in Christ for the synoptic idea of the kingdom. From this point of view it is possible to say that the age of the kingdom is equivalent to the era of the church, though the kingdom has not yet come in its fulness.

The ethics of Christ are the ethics of the kingdom. Christians are members of the kingdom, if they are in Christ, but yet the kingdom still lies in the future. Christians are therefore men of two aeons, both saved and in process of being saved, always trying to 'become what we are' in the midst of the pressures of a world which is very far from being the kingdom of God. Hence the ethical teachings of Jesus, in so far as they continue to be applicable, become ideals rather than rules for the normal ordering of life. The ambiguous position of the Christian has always been the cause of a certain moral tension between the ideal and the practicable. One solution was the 'double standard' of the Middle Ages, but that was frankly a farce, as the monks and hermits were by no means all saints, in spite of their consecration to the 'higher' way of life (if it really is higher). Protestantism rightly rejected this view, which fatally reduces the incentive to the rest of society to try to live the Christian life. But from the point of view of the individual today, the tension between Christian ideals and life in a secular world remains unresolved. And ideals can have little moral effect unless some way can be found of making them impinge directly on the realities of life.

## V

It is now high time to say something constructive after exposing so many difficulties. A critical view of the Bible tends to undermine its privileged position as a guide to ethics. The Bible as a whole can scarcely be used in this way. The teaching of Jesus presents formidable problems when taken simply as a book of rules. The attempt to discover a single principle in his teaching (*agape*) is also open to objections. Recent work on christology is also unhelpful at first sight. If all the emphasis is placed upon the humanity of Jesus, his teaching is easily warped into social idealism or dissolved into existentialism. But the quasi-atheism which lies behind these assessments is not necessarily the consequence of New Testament criticism. The task of exegesis is to uncover what Jesus was really saying and doing, and there is no need to jettison the theism which is his absolutely unquestioned presupposition, and which alone gives his work its true meaning according to his own valuation of it. Nevertheless his preaching of the kingdom had to be reinterpreted in terms of 'being in Christ' in the first generation of Christian living. The tension between the high standard which this entails and the realities of life in the world has never been satisfactorily resolved.

A way through the impasse may be found by listening sympathetically to one of the humanist objections to Christian faith. It is asserted that reliance on God, or on the Bible as the Word of God, is to some extent a retreat from full moral responsibility. A mature person will discover his moral principles within himself. In the last analysis his moral decisions are his own, and he must be prepared to take the consequences of them. Moreover the range of ethical questions is so vast that it is impossible to expect an ancient collection of literature like the Bible to provide all the answers or even the necessary principles for them.

If we are prepared to admit the truth of this, we shall see that one matter is of first-rate importance, and that is the education of the person to play such a responsible role. This is not simply a matter of school-education, but of deepening thought and awareness throughout life. From this point of view the Christian will seek to deepen his own moral awareness by recourse to the central truths of his faith. He may garner much help from many of the great ethical writings of world literature, but it is to the Bible that he will turn first and foremost. For there is contained the experience of the people of God, to which he himself belongs through his membership in Christ. He will recognize that the Bible cannot solve all his moral problems for him, but he will be better equipped to tackle them himself, because of the biblical formation of his mind.

For the purposes of systematic ethics, it is already clear enough that the Bible cannot be taken *en bloc* as revealed law to set over against natural law. Really it is a mistake to regard the two as opposites. In so far as there is such a thing as natural law, it is revealed through nature, and the Bible, as a special record of men's experience of God, confirms it, and indicates its true status. If the duty of Christians has some features which go beyond the natural law, this is because the Christian life, as a response to God's saving action in Christ, brings into play a special range of moral issues. But these cannot conflict with the natural law, because on a theistic view God is the author of both. But just as the Bible fails to give a coherent revealed law, but the ethics of Christ has to be dug out by careful critical work and related to the salvation-event, so the Bible is not an infallible guide to natural law, but rather an assembly of the variegated possibilities which follow from the theistic presupposition. The authority of the Bible stands upon its own merits rather than on a privileged position. We can be prepared to find it mistaken in some ways. That will not detract from its continuing claim to be heeded.

# 7

# How we make Moral Decisions

## DON CUPITT

### I. ETHICS AND MORALS

Let us begin with some definitions. By the term *morals* I mean the everyday business of making and implementing practical decisions as to our conduct, in small matters and great – both snap decisions and shifts in long-term policy such as decisions about employment or basic allegiances. A morality, or moral code, is a more or less systematic body of principles upon which such decisions are made. When we talk of moral experience, or of a man of strong moral principles, or of a moral order in one's life, the term *moral* has this practical sense.

By the term *ethics*, on the other hand, I mean a commentary upon morality – the theoretical study of the nature of moral acts, language, decisions and experience. For example, discussion of the formal structure of moral language and analysis of the use of such terms as *right* and *good* is part of ethics. Ethics is the philosophy of morals. It is often called *moral philosophy*, but I would prefer to avoid using that term on the same grounds as I would prefer to avoid *religious philosophy* or *scientific philosophy*. By speaking rather of philosophy of religion and philosophy of science one stresses that there is nothing specially religious or scientific about the philosophizing, but only about the subject-matter of that act. Similarly, moral philosophy is ordinary philosophizing about morality, not moralizing philosophy.

Ordinary usage is roughly – but only roughly – in line with my distinction. If I speak of Kant's ethics you will probably take me to refer to Kant's writings on ethics, whereas if I speak of Kant's morals I suppose I might be understood to be speaking of his habits of conduct. On the other hand, if we distinguish medical ethics from the morals of doctors we are distinguishing public or official from private conduct – a different distinction.

It is common nowadays to stress the moral neutrality of ethics, in that the doing of ethics is not logically connected with the adoption or endorsement of any particular moral code. Within limits, this is quite proper. But it would be odd if the writer of Kant's ethics had the morals urged upon his son by the second earl of Chesterfield. Everyone who does ethics is also a moral agent, and every moral agent is willy-nilly involved in questions of ethics.

Suppose, for example, that someone is trying to argue me into a certain course of action. On such an occasion people employ very compressed phrases such as, 'After all, he *is* your brother', 'How would *you* like . . . ?', 'What if everyone . . . ?', 'Well, you must just act for the best', or 'It's your decision, and I can't make it for you. But don't forget that . . .'. Such phrases could almost be described as embodying ethical theories *in nuce*. I may find one phrase generally more compelling or persuasive than another, or more persuasive in one particular instance than another. At this point, surely, morals and ethics are interwoven. I may be most deeply impressed by the pointing out of relevant facts; by the appeal to the example or wishes of some venerated person; by the appeal to consequences. One of these types of argument may be apt on one occasion, and another more suitable on some other occasion. If I am in general most impressed by the appeal to consequences in moral argument it is to be expected that I will be a utilitarian in ethics. My account of the nature of moral language and argument will appeal to, and generalize on the basis of, the kind of persuasions which I feel to be most telling in matters of morals. My ethical utilitarianism will show some signs of strain as I stretch it to accommodate and account for cases of moral argument which appear *prima facie* to fit better with a deontological ethical theory. In fact moral experience and the formation of our moral characters are so complex that Sidgwick and others have doubted whether there can be a complete ethical theory.

Lastly, by *the metaphysics of morals* (a term invented by Kant) I mean enquiry as to the relevance of ethics and morals to metaphysics – a general account of the nature of reality. Does moral experience or ethical theory suggest any metaphysical doctrine? The metaphysics of morals may include a justification of morality, or a proof of some ethical theory: but then again no such thing may be necessary. Those who would make the distinction between morality and ethics most sharply would usually maintain that all attempts at a metaphysical justification of morality are superfluous and must contain a fallacy. Those who ask, 'Why should I be moral?', don't understand the meaning of the words.

The true position seems to be as follows. It is true that there are no *formal* logical relations between moral statements on the one hand and statements of fact or of metaphysical or religious belief on the other. But it is wrong to conclude that there are therefore no logical relations whatever between these various sorts of statements. On the contrary there are rich and intricate informal logical relations between them.

## II. THE A POSTERIORI METHOD

In talking of morals, it may be said, I have failed to distinguish study of what is the case from study of what ought to be the case about people's moral thinking and conduct. One ought to distinguish descriptive and normative studies. But I am not sure that we can be too hard-and-fast here. Argument in moral philosophy is largely conducted by citing examples, that is, by appealing to common experience. In different ways Butler, Hume and Mill all state that they will appeal direct to moral experience and seem deliberately to override the distinction to which I have just referred.

Butler says that the *a posteriori* method in ethics, which asks 'what the particular nature of man is' and 'what course of life it is, which is correspondent to this whole nature', 'is in a peculiar manner adapted to satisfy a fair mind'. So he adopts this method in his Sermons as being the most suitable for his audience.[1]

Hume proposes to unveil the origin of morals by asking what moral qualities people in fact approve or disapprove. 'As this is a question of fact . . . we can only expect success by following the experimental method and deducing [*sic*] general maxims from a comparison of particular instances.'[2] Butler, and Hume (with less enthusiasm), both acknowledge the possibility of the *a priori* method, but they prefer the other.

Mill goes further, for he holds that no other method than the *a posteriori* is possible, and points in evidence to what he regards as Kant's failure to do anything useful with his highly general *a priori* principles. He insists that 'the sole evidence it is possible to produce that anything is desirable, is that people do actually desire it'.[3] Mill's argument has been much criticized, as turning upon an equivocation between two utterly distinct meanings of desirable, namely capable-of-being-desired and worthy-of-being desired. But the criticism begs the question which Mill asks. He denies that the two meanings are utterly distinct. And where else *can* you start from but the facts?

It is worth recalling that people ordinarily think of themselves as doing, most of the time, what they ought to be doing. For example, in many occupations one may at any time be required to account for one's actions, to produce the books or to submit to inspection. The inspection may be very minute and the standards expected very high. The speech for the defence, the *apologia* or autobiography, is one of the fundamental types of human utterance. Certainly study of ethics must include consideration of the very varied types of justification of their own conduct which people offer. It is odd that so often the logic of moral discourse as a species of normative language is discussed without, it would seem, any concrete grasp of the facts of moral discourse. The examples are wooden and the psychology and sociology of morals are ignored. In justification we are offered an isolated sentence from Hume, a criticism of Mill, an argument from G. E. Moore and an axiom about the moral neutrality of ethics. But all four of these items are questionable.

Locke and his successors, the British empiricists, were fond of inviting us to lift our heads from their pages, sit back and try a little psychological experiment. Why should we not do the same, recording and reflecting upon the actual moral cases with which we have had to deal?

## III. Four Cases

A. To adopt my own suggestion, two paragraphs ago I was interrupted in the composition of this paper. I was told that someone wished to call on me, and was waiting at the College gate. On enquiry I found that his claim was very slight. He gave his name, stated that he had met me a number of years ago, and was paying a social call. The courtesy of the request was itself a claim – civility ought to be met with civility. But I was irritated at being interrupted, and then dismissed the irritation as the academic's childish selfishness. I asked him in, we talked for an hour, and then, I must confess, I edged him out.

What happens in such a case? The practical decisions are made, not individually but almost jointly, in the intercourse of persons.

Many things pass through one's mind. There is the religious force of the claim which someone's arrival makes, and there are the claims of civility. There are of course men of great moral seriousness who are entirely without civility; and, trying though this deficiency is, such men are greatly to be preferred to those of great civility who have no morals. Nevertheless civility *is* important, and religion makes it more so. But there was also my irritation at being interrupted in a task such as I require some effort of will to persevere in, reinforced by a touch of scepticism. Why does a stranger, who happens to be in the town, call in this way? What is his object? When it turns out that his object is merely reminiscence I become restless. I do not love reminiscence. I am barely more hospitable than common decency dictates.

In my hesitation about whether to ask the stranger in I behaved in an oddly mechanical way, in the sense that I could almost have represented diagrammatically the forces inclining me to act one way or another. The vectors tugging in different directions resolved themselves after a few moments of uncomfortable hesitation into a resultant decision, with a slight sighing explosion of relief. One lengthens the first syllable of one's next utterance, saying something like, 'Oh well!', 'All right', 'Send him in'. Then, after the meeting and the first exchanges of signals, by which the terms of a conversation are established and the participants settle down, there follows after an interval that stage where both parties are torn between an effort to attend and their searching for the opportune moment to lean forward, knock out their pipes, emit a short barking laugh, and rise. There is a curious consent about this, easily achieved where both are speaking their native language, but at other times often comically difficult to arrive at. Then, when both have risen, they feel slightly ashamed of their haste and the unsatisfactory nature of the meeting. They linger at the door, and even become effusive in the effort to strike a spark of real warmth; so that, in the end, they have to repeat the rituals by which a conversation is terminated.

In such an encounter one notices the competing considerations of convenience, civility and morality, and notices that they correspond pretty much to Butler's self-love, benevolence and conscience, albeit at a rather trivial level. More importantly, one notices that in such moral situations decisions are not taken and acted upon independently. Instead a mutuality is established in which one acts by consent, as in dancing. One is not recollected into oneself and does not decide of oneself: any decision must be signalled and acted upon collaboratively.

Stern moralists have often, to their loss, disparaged and neglected consideration of manners.

Still thinking about my conduct to my late visitor – about which I am becoming increasingly uneasy; but more of this unease in a moment – I see the irrelevance of brandishing a phrase like *free-will* if I wish that it had been different. People say, had I chosen to act differently I would have acted differently, and no doubt that is true enough, but it is not very much to the point. If two people fail to hit it off, to establish a *rapport* quickly, no amount of offering whisky instead of coffee (or nothing) is going to alter the impression their conversation leaves. Our characters are what they are, and make themselves felt almost whatever our words and gestures may be. And the appeal to free-will can easily overlook the collaborative element in such a situation.

As for my unease, it arises as follows: When I think of my character I must distinguish my character as it is from my character as I would like to think of it. I must distinguish my actual self from my ego-ideal, but not separate them. When my behaviour falls conspicuously short of my ego-ideal I feel uneasy. I have a bad conscience, I feel inwardly divided. I fall in my own estimation. Undoubtedly in the business of living our most important ethical motive is the need constantly to hold together our actual characters and our own ego-ideals. The more successful we are in this, the stronger our characters. We seek in each occasion the compromise – such as my own very moderate degree of hospitality just now – which will neither do undue violence to our instincts nor betray our ideals. One must count the cost; it is foolish to make greater demands upon oneself than one is likely to be able to bear: but on the other hand if I altogether betray my ego-ideal I suffer a loss of sense of my own value so mortifying as to make me of little use in life at all. My actual character and my ego-ideal must maintain a tolerable working relationship: they must even be reciprocally adapted. And so they come to be, for the most part.

My character and my ego-ideal are formed and in formation as a result of influences almost too numerous to specify. In such matters as family relations, child-rearing, the handling of money and domestic affairs we re-enact our parents' characters and attitudes to a remarkable degree, so that a reflective person constantly has the experience of *déjà-vu*. Genius is total recall of childhood, and self-knowledge the awareness of one's child-self. In the public realm one's conduct very largely reflects the *ethos* and fulfils the expectations of the various groups to which one has belonged or now belongs – schools, the armed forces, trade or profession, class, nationality, and religious, political and cultural associations. To look at a man's *curriculum vitae* is after all to have a rough notion of what he is. And if we are more than the sum of these influences upon us we can hardly know what we are that is more until we have accepted and understood their power.

B. Two days ago I was charged too little in a shop. I realized the fact as I turned from the counter to leave, and felt at once a jump of anxiety. I might have been apprehensive because the suggestion presented itself that I could say nothing and leave, or because I had to decide within two or three seconds whether to stay or leave. It might have been the temptation, or the freedom, which alarmed me. In fact I called back the assistant and paid the difference. Why this particular resolution of a conflict? Considerations of various kinds passed before my mind. I recalled an occasion when at the age of ten or so I stole a Chelsea bun from the baker – we were rather hungry at boarding-school in 1945 – and the memory was as important to me as his apples were to St Augustine. There is a suggestion here that I felt the after-echo of an accusing voice from childhood. I think there was an element of pride, in that I made a little display of my gratuitous honesty. And I thought also that if one grumbles at shop-assistants who – presumably inadvertently – return too little change, it is only fair that one point out the occasion when one is given too much change.

But in such a case it is not easy to distinguish the rational and specifically moral element in a decision from the emotional factors. I do not see how I could decide whether I paid up for duty's sake, for I do not see how I could retrospectively determine whether the motive of reverence for the moral law was present in sufficient force to have brought about my decision independently of the various emotional and indeed autobiographical factors involved. Indeed it's not quite clear how the motive of reverence for the moral law can be distinguished as a motive from other motives, for if it is a motive among other motives its strength relative to the other motives is what it is and it becomes difficult to retain any meaning for the claim that I could have decided otherwise. If the various vectors tugging away from a point are each what they are, what sense does it make to say that the resultant could be other than it is? And can reverence for the moral law as such be distinguished from reverence for the persons who taught it to one? If one can make such a distinction in thought, does it matter that one cannot make it in the concrete? At any rate we are faced with the possibility that we can never know whether we have ever performed an entirely morally good action. Why is it that, on reflection, one welcomes the suggestion? I suppose it is because ethical theories which concentrate attention on motives may easily make us anxious and scrupulous. Our motives seem to get more mixed the more we examine them, so that self-knowledge is always bad news. It would be a relief to draw a clearer line between motives and intentions and apply moral terms only to the latter.

To my mind the likeliest interpretation of the present case is that I tried out imaginatively in my mind the two possibilities before me. I put on successively like garments myself paying up and myself walking out of the shop – though not, of course, in that order, for the temptation (that is, the anxiety-provoking suggestion) always comes first. At any rate, I could not see myself doing the latter, that is, I did not like the thought of myself as the sort of person who would do the latter. The suggestion was damaging to my self-esteem. Here's the element of pride. By so acting I would have betrayed my ego-ideal. I couldn't live with myself with a clear conscience if I had to accept that I was the sort of person who would be mean in so petty a way. The trivial sum involved made things worse. I did not care to make *that* into part of the truth about myself, and of course we do make much of that truth which we are so reluctant to face. On the other hand the self-image of punctilious and even pedantic honesty suggested by staying put and paying up was gratifying. The gain in morale was cheap at the price: indeed the pettiness of the sum involved was an added attraction.

Careful self-scrutiny as to one's motives is something undertaken so rarely that we easily think it pathological – a symptom of anxiety, or of a morbid introspectiveness. At any rate the outcome is familiarly discouraging. Do we not in fact regard careful examination into motives as being morally enervating or even damaging? There do seem to be areas where a certain unthinking simplicity and spontaneity is humanly necessary, and too careful an examination of the act is somehow destructive of its human worth. To say this is not to say that the traditional ideal of the fully examined life is worthless, but simply to point out that the examination may in some cases alter the character of, and even damage, what is examined. There *is* a sense in which an act or a decision must be unthinking, in order to be fresh and clean. It is perhaps at this point that Jesus and Paul rebuke the Pharisees, and a certain hard-edged rationalism in ethics must give place to religious immediacy. But it is painful to recall that the revival of the doctrine of justification by faith alone in Protestantism did not always set people free from scrupulosity and moralism.

C. The case I have just described is in its way complex enough. The properly moral core of it was no doubt the admission that it is only fair to own up when one is undercharged if one would have complained had one been overcharged. But this admission could itself be developed along several different lines; for example in terms of Kant's first formulation of the categorical imperative, in utilitarian terms, or in terms of a notion of natural justice – notice the force of the word *only* in the preceding sentence. But in other respects the case is exceptionally simple. The instantaneous presentation of a clear dilemma is not a common experience.

For example, of late I have been thinking that my present annual charitable subscription by deed of covenant to an organization working for the relief of hunger overseas is much too small. The thought has indeed crossed my mind from time to time during the past two or three years, but without result. Yet how can one fail to make a simple arrangement by which much distress is relieved at negligible cost to oneself? The very ease with which the decision makes itself seems to militate against actually implementing it. I am so convinced about the matter that I leave the implementation to look after itself. Indeed the only reasons why I have now done something about it are that my wife has shamed me by mentioning the matter again, and that it occurred to me as an example in the preparation of this paper. Until then no situation had arisen which had precipitated the matter.

No doubt prudent organizers of charitable subscriptions have these traits of human nature in mind when they advertise their intention to publish the names of donors and the amounts of their donations upon a certain day. The ostensible reason for doing this is that donors shall be assured that the fund is honestly administered, and this reason is allowed to cloak the one which is less comfortable to acknowledge. Nevertheless the latter consideration does its work in the obscure region where practical decisions are made and acted upon, stimulating potential donors and counter-acting their tendency to defer performance of actions already in principle decided upon.

Whereas in our reflections upon the last case we were led to consider the limits of the utility of habits of self-examination and observance of moral rules, in this present case we see an instance of their value. Self-examination may clog the springs of action, but it may also cut away self-deceit and indolence. It is a double-edged instrument.

It is worth noticing that, important as a discipline of self-knowledge is in any morality (and, in view of what we have said, important as it is to acknowledge its dangers) the kind of self-knowledge which is relevant to morality does not seem to have anything epistemologically privileged about it. If I say that I have long meant to increase that subscription but have not yet got around to doing so, and you smile to yourself, you smile only because for a moment you know me better than I know myself. You observe the speciousness of my excuse, and you guess that if I were to pause for a moment I would half admit its speciousness myself. In fact self-knowledge in morals is not a kind of knowledge of ourselves which is private to us and more immediate than any other person can ever have; on the contrary it is merely the kind of knowledge of ourselves which our shrewd friends have of us. Presumably the self-knowledge gained by undergoing psychoanalysis is also no more than learning to see ourselves as the analyst can see us. Self-knowledge in morality is to see ourselves as others see us: to take the generality of moral principles seriously and cease to make an exception of ourselves in a way which we instantly reprehend in others.

D. A fourth and last example of an actual moral case is that which arises when I ask myself, what kind of person am I becoming, and do I wish to be? I am 33 years old at the time of writing (1967), and have recently met again some of those who were my contemporaries as students. Thirty-three was the age at which Jesuits were (inaccurately, I am told) supposed to begin their life-work, and Jesus had ended his. It is nearly half the allotted span, old enough for some of one's contemporaries to have made a real mark in the world, and for others to have suffered disastrously. My friends and I look at each other with amusement, in the case of the well-mannered, or coarse laughter, in the case of the ill-mannered, at what we have

become. We are beginning to set firm into moulds which are a kind
of bad caricature of what we were, or professed to be, in our youth.
By a series of small compromises our ideals and opinions are being
carefully adjusted to fit the facts of what we are. They sit on us now
more gracefully. If we are more cynical, we are more harmonious.
Our discontent and our happinesses are less extreme than they were,
and this makes for more comfort. What is more, to some slight
extent we have adjusted not only our ideals to ourselves, but ourselves to our ideals. This is creditable, though the embodiment is
seldom quite so unambiguously edifying as its precursor in ideal. We
expose our ideals to mockery as we come to embody them.

As we have grown less aggressively critical of our seniors, so we
have come to demand less of ourselves, by a *quid pro quo*. But we
are aware that as the reservoir of unfulfilled future possibilities
drains, we are less able to vindicate ourselves prospectively by appealing to what we promise to achieve one day. We are thrown upon
and obliged to reckon with what we already are, as our space for
manoeuvre becomes more restricted. Thus the question of what kind
of person I am has become more embarrassing, and that of what
kind of person I should like to become more poignant, than formerly.

Questions of this sort are not very convincingly answered in
terms of some classical ethical theories. Should I like to be a person
who unfailingly observes a number of rules, or a person who always
so acts as to maximize happiness? Popular psychologizing tells me
to try to become more and more myself, but I suspect that I am all
too much myself already, and will certainly become more so without
any extraordinary exertions.

A more apt answer to the question of what I am to become is in
terms less of the moral act than in terms of the moral life, of the
virtues. Virtues are habits, and I am increasingly a creature of habit.
Habits are comfortable, so that even habitual discomfort can be
more comfortable than unpredictable comforts. In the larger area of
moral decision which we are now considering what moves us most
effectively is the appeal of certain qualities of character as embodied
in an exemplar to whom we owe an habitual allegiance.

The allegiance of a settled man is not at all the same thing as the
hero-worship of unsettled men who study to copy the very manner-
isms of their hero. There are many ways in which one can be related
to the model, and of them all perhaps hero-worship is the most

deceitful. In retrospect it can look ludicrously false both to its object and to itself. But the power of moral example can survive this disillusionment. There is nothing immature in the way a man like Kierkegaard writes of Christ as the pattern.

By the way, we have here an explanation of the moral function performed by certain religious doctrines which have often seemed morally objectionable – I mean doctrines of universal sinfulness, of God's absolute holiness before which we are for ever dust, of the 'teleological suspension of the ethical'. For as I settle I need more of a shaking to move me. I need settled moral principles, but I also need symbols with the power to relativize my morality and even to overthrow it so that I can start afresh. My moral constitution usually needs only amendments but it may on occasion need revolution.

I have cited four actual cases of moral decision so as to show something of their range. No doubt the range could have been wider, and no doubt the cases chosen are a sample biased by the special peculiarities of the only person about whom I am qualified to write. But at least they are actual cases.

## IV. MORAL EXPERIENCE AND ETHICAL THEORIES

Some moral cases lend themselves to interpretation in terms of more than one ethical theory. Other cases are more readily amenable to interpretation in terms of one ethical theory than of others. Most ethical theories attempt to subsume the whole of our moral experience under a single formal pattern, and show greater or less degrees of straining in the attempt to do so.

For example, Deontological Ethical Theories, in which the concept of obligation is supreme, relate to a situation where we find ourselves obliged to choose, and know that a moral principle which we have previously adopted bears unambiguously upon the case. We know, in the light of moral policy decisions which we have already made, and moral principles which are part of us, what we ought to do. The question is only whether we shall do it. In such a case the recognition of obligation, authoritativeness, is very commonly mistaken for an *intuition* of a transcendent moral order of things, or even a revelation of the will of God. Its peremptory and overriding quality has been stressed in a way which divorces it from the facts. It is thought to be unconditional and timeless. I believe this to be an unnecessary supposition. The authoritativeness and obligatoriness lie in the unambiguous clarity and force with which my present moral makeup and policy tells me what I ought to do. Conscience is the voice of my ego-ideal. If I say, 'Jones can be implicitly trusted to do X,' or, 'Smith would never do Y,' I mean that the characters of Jones and Smith are such that, confronted with X and Y respectively, I know what they will do, I know how they will react. To do not-X, or to do Y would contradict all I know about Jones and Smith. Therein lies the obligatoriness. Jones just cannot see himself doing not-X and Smith is just not the man to do Y. The bindingness of the imperatives they feel relates to their own established characters rather than to an intuition from on high. None of us would have such an intuition in relation to a quite novel kind of moral case. On the contrary, that is where we should feel most uncertain.

And Teleological Ethical Theories relate especially to this latter kind of case, where we are not so much trying to decide to do what we already know to be right, but trying to decide what is right. We are in a state of moral perplexity. It is not immediately evident to us what we ought to do. The growth of our moral characters is like the growth of a great body of case law, and the situation we are now considering is one where, for various reasons, our previous experience and decisions provide no clear guidance. The case may be novel. It may be one in which there is a conflict of duties. It may be very complex – with many imponderable factors. At any rate, in such a case there is nothing else to do except weigh the pros and cons and act for the best. The highly complex decisions which men have to make in public life are very largely of this kind.

So the main interest of deontological theories is in the morality of *agents* and the main interest of teleological theories is in the morality of *acts*. Each urges against the other that it is hopelessly difficult to apply. How can we really know our motives? How can we calculate consequences?

It is common to suggest that all ethical theories may be reduced to variants of these two. This seems to be an oversimplification. The case discussed in III(D) above is an example of a large class of cases relating to one's whole scheme of values – decisions about one's marriage, career, or political or religious allegiances. In this area of moral thinking the emphasis is more upon the moral life than the motives of the agent or the consequences of his act. A *Weltanschauung*, a whole way of thinking is at stake. In this sense morality does in the end lead us to ask metaphysical or religious questions.

There is a curious manoeuvre common among philosophers of

either restricting or broadening the connotation of a word well beyond its ordinary commonsense limits in order to produce an illuminating paradox. For example, many philosophers since Plato have proposed so strictly defined a meaning for the word *knowledge* as to make it seem that we hardly know anything at all except truisms. At the other extreme, someone may broaden the connotation of the word *mad* by saying, 'We are all mad really', meaning, I suppose, that the distinction between madness and sanity is none too clear-cut. It would be absurd if we allowed these paradoxes to undermine our conviction that the sun will rise tomorrow morning, and that we can tell a sane man from a madman. There is no clear-cut distinction between hot and cold, but I know what difference it makes whether you tell me that the bathwater is too hot or it is too cold.

If philosophers of morals assert that all cases of moral decision can be analysed without remainder in terms of intuited obligation, or that they can all be analysed in terms of calculated felicificity, then they are performing a similar manoeuvre. Such a manoeuvre may be useful and illuminating, but one should not be misled by it. The facts are more complicated. It is not surprising that in the Christian tradition, where we find a rich and various family of styles of moral persuasion, we have something too complex to analyse in terms of a single ethical theory. Throughout the Bible appeal to purity of heart, the deontological theme, runs together with the insistence upon fruits or works, the teleological theme. Even in the Torah, so often misrepresented as a catalogue of arbitrary decrees, the variety of styles of moral persuasion will astonish the careful reader: imitation of the divine holiness or justice, apt response to the patterns of divine actions, appeals to sympathy, to custom, to venerated example, to natural justice, to prudence, to conscience – all these are to be found. A great moral tradition has a complex logic. It is itself a culture – a group with a rich *ethos* influencing the lives of its members. This paper has shown, I hope, that I do not think the Christian has in any simple sense supernatural guidance in the making, or assistance in the implementation, of moral decisions. Nor do I think ethical theories are the sole source of such guidance or assistance. The guidance and assistance is to be sought in ourselves, and in the culture and allegiances which we each have. The Christian's approach to ethics is conditioned by the special kind of culture and the special allegiances he has as a Christian.

# 8

# God and Morality

## DON CUPITT

In this paper I shall explore the material relation between religious belief and moral conduct. I shall not be primarily concerned with the question of the logical relation between theology and ethics. On that topic I agree with A. C. Ewing[1] that both ethics and theology benefit from a measure of formal independence. Each is then free to influence the other. If one were definable in terms of the other it would be hard to see how moral criticism of religious beliefs and religious criticism of morality could both be so fruitful as they have been. Formal independence needs to be maintained: but on the other hand, plainly, a man's religious beliefs or disbeliefs do affect his moral thinking. How?

That there is an intimate relation between religious belief and moral conduct is clearly maintained by the New Testament writers. C. H. Dodd has drawn attention to the resounding 'therefore' which marks St Paul's transition from doctrinal exposition to moral instruction.[2] Again, in the letter commonly called 'I John', the writer seems almost to hold that there is a formal relation between the propositions 'God is love', 'We ought to love God' and 'We ought to love the brethren'. You cannot truly assent to one without assenting to the others.[3]

So for the NT writers it would seem that the conduct-patterns of Christian virtue are to be construed as a fitting response to, and expression of, the Christian experience of God. That is to say, the basic imagery through which God is thought is already partly practical. It evokes a net of moral relations. For example, to call God 'Father' is to be committed to certain moral attitudes: regarding other men as brothers, holding that no man should have *absolute* power over another man, responding to God in religion in some ways rather than others.

This accounts for the otherwise curious fact that questions about God's existence and questions about his goodness are almost always taken together. People are not willing to believe in God unless they feel they have reason to believe that he is good. *Religious* belief that there is a God includes belief that he is good.

Notice that the practical utility of social imagery presupposes some recognition of natural human morality, even though some theologians have been reluctant to admit it. For presumably we must be able to judge what the relations between fathers and sons, and between brothers, ought to be like if we are to regard these relations as religiously suggestive – suggestive that is of what the relations between men under God ought to be like. It would be odd to hold *both* that our moral judgments about natural fatherhood, brother-hood and sonship are disordered or defective *and* that though defective they are none the less apt images of our relation to God. But to notice this oddity is precisely to have evinced a conviction that there are indeed profound affinities between our moral and our religious beliefs. It would seem that the more adequate our grasp of moral truth, the more adequate our grasp of religious truth.

Now in all such arguments two premises will, I think, almost invariably be found to be present, either singly or in combination. They are (i) that we ought to imitate God, and (ii) that we ought to respond to God in the ways which are suggested by the imagery through which we think him. I shall call these the *imitation* theme and the *response* theme.

The best example available to show the deep interplay of these two themes in our moral formation is the fact that we each have two parents, one who is of our own sex, and one who is of the 'opposite' sex. In order to grow properly into my gender identity I need both a parent of the same sex upon whom to model myself and *vis-à-vis* whom I am in one sort of tension, and a parent of the opposite sex who gives me my gender identity by antithesis, by being not like me, and *vis-à-vis* whom I am in a quite different sort of tension. If I am deprived of either of these relations I am liable to suffer some deformation. Thus the formation of our personalities *vis-à-vis* our parents is a complex and beautiful interweaving of patterns of imitation and response. In order to get a proper sense of ourselves we need to be able to measure ourselves both against what is like us and against what is unlike us.

In ethical theism God is believed to play both parts – he leads us on by being both like us and unlike us, so that it is a kind of blasphemy to suppose that he has sexuality and so needs a consort to complement him in the spiritual formation of mankind. The reasons why masculine gender has been attributed to him are another story.

Some Christian theologians are critical of any suggestion that the imitation of God plays a large part in Christian ethics.[4] However, it is plainly an important theme in the Old Testament. The impartiality and the justice of God are an example to judges, his mercy to Israel when she was an alien in Egypt is an example for Israel's treatment of aliens. His people are to be holy as he is holy, merciful as he is merciful, righteous as he is righteous. The notion that the imitation of the gods is the most blessed form of life appears both in Plato and Aristotle, and was commonly used as a proof of the superiority of the contemplative over the active life, since the gods were blessed, and their business was contemplation. In the New Testament the demand to imitate the divine perfection is of course heard in the Sermon on the Mount,[5] but more often the pattern is of the form, the believer should mimic Christ who is the image of God; or even of the form, the believer should mimic the apostle, who mimics Christ, who is the image of God. Or it may be that we should express it like this – with the divine Spirit's help the believer mimics God's condescending love for men exhibited in Christ.[6] But however you put it, the notion of the imitation of God is still there. Jesus Christ, the God-man, is interpolated between God and the believer in order to ease the undoubted difficulties in the concept of *imitatio Dei*, but he cannot abolish them, for he is a man and to believe in him as the true image of God must be to believe that at least *he* imitated God, that there can be some representation of God in human life.

And the notion of the imitation of God is full of difficulties. Historically it has led to ideals in spirituality which now seem repugnant: that of *apatheia*, a sort of human equivalent of God's impassibility, for example. When fathers of families start playing God they are not always admirable.

A more profound difficulty is that you can only make the imitation of God, or of God in Christ, a fundamental motive in human morality if you suppose that God is a kind of moral agent. And this is very odd indeed. How can God be supposed a social being, or subject to moral obligation or to temptation? How can he be called morally free? There is a curious difficulty in Christian thought here. For theology obviously does not wish God to be supposed morally free in the same sense that men are. It would be a kind of contradiction to suggest that God is free to sin. Theology seems to require a highly analogical concept of moral freedom in order to distinguish the senses in which freedom is predicated of God, the blessed in heaven, men on earth and so on.

And yet God is credited with a kind of work of supererogation in redeeming us. Prayers and Christian writings suggest that we should be more thankful for our redemption than for our creation. It is as if God could, without laying himself open to criticism, have left us in our sins. Nothing obliged him to redeem us. Indeed, he would have been entirely just in condemning us. But he freely chose to treat us better than we really deserved. He did more than he need have done. If creation is a work of grace, then redemption is grace upon grace.

Thus this sort of Christian talk actually goes so far as to suggest what seems to be a distinction something like that between natural moral virtue and supernatural moral virtue *in God*! Such a distinction must be supposed if it is reasonable to be more astonished and grateful for redemption than for creation, and must in some sense be supposed in any account of grace.

What is more, God's act of surpassing himself in this way (or at least, surpassing what we have a right to expect of him) is held to be the foundation of Christian morality as a morality of love, *agape*. For *agape* is precisely that moral principle which transcends and may even seem to subvert ordinary morality, which justifies the ungodly, and forgives the unforgivable; which in all ages men have discerned in the story of Christ. The contemplation of the divine *agape* generates in us, by way of response and imitation, the characteristically Christian spirit of thanksgiving (eucharist) and generous love.

It would seem then impossible to deny that the imitation of God *does* play a central part in Christian morality. To show *agape* is to surpass oneself and so mimic God's surpassing love. There have been theologians, such as William of Ockham, who have objected to the anthropormorphism of this. But their alternative account of Christian ethics, which founded it not upon the imitation of his nature but upon obedience to the positive and inscrutable decree of his will, is itself exposed to still more damaging criticism.

As for the response theme in Christian ethics, it presents fewer difficulties. For it is commonly held nowadays that to believe that *p* is to be disposed to act as if *p*. There are no doubt defects in this analysis,[7] but they can be made up to some extent in the case of religious beliefs. For we have seen that since the imagery through which God is thought is social and moral, to affirm the imagery is already to acknowledge a duty to behave in certain ways. And it is an accepted idiom to say that a man doesn't *really* believe in the love of God if his conduct is not accordant with that belief.

It would seem then that we *are* getting a glimpse by now of the shape of the informal logical relation between religious beliefs and moral conduct. But now another problem presents itself. It is that of the odd looseness of this relation, and it can be shown in two ways.

In the first place, the same moral principles can be held to follow from contradictory premisses. For example, St John argues that because we have a God who is love, and has shown his love by the gift of his Son, we ought to love one another. But Richard Robinson, no doubt in conscious defiance of this argument, argues that because there is no one in heaven to love us and we are alone together in an indifferent universe, it is therefore all the more necessary that we love one another.[8]

In the second place, highly divergent moral attitudes can be held to follow from the same theological premisses. For example, the very specific theology of apocalyptic originates or is revived in certain specifiable social conditions at many places and times, but the moral lessons it is used to inculcate may vary greatly. The theological message is that though the times are evil, God is ready, the end is near and he will vindicate his elect. The moral conclusion may be, in the book of Daniel, steadfast endurance of persecution; among the Qumran sect, military preparedness and even military revolt; in Paul, quietness, moderation and vigilance; in Thomas Münzer, armed insurrection; in *Uncle Tom's Cabin*, Sunday consolation; but to a later age of American Negroes, marches and civil disobedience.

An additional complication is this: as time passes a religious tradition gathers breadth and diversity. The range of ideal forms of life in Christianity, even among the religious orders alone, is remarkable. In time the extreme diversity of the tradition tends to encourage eclecticism. Each man makes his own personal anthology from the

tradition, gathering those elements which accord with his circumstances and tastes. There are world-affirming and world-renouncing
elements in Christianity: elements to suit people who see things
in black and white, and elements to suit people who see things in
shades of grey: elements to suit men of principle who see life in
terms of the fulfilment of duties, and elements to suit men of
spontaneity who believe in the unique moment; individualist and
corporatist elements; authoritative and anarchic elements. There's a
place for the once-born and a place for the twice-born, and a place
for every political opinion ever held.

It's all very well to talk of family resemblances, but there is a
danger that the family will become so large that it includes every
way of life that conscientious men have ever thought admirable and
there will be no point in talking of a distinctively Christian morality
at all, because it will exclude almost nothing.

So although we can describe the Christian moral temper in a way
which seems fairly specific and will (we hope) evoke general agreement, when we endeavour to translate it into specific policies and
ways of life, anarchy prevails. For this reason many Christian
moralists have talked of the need for intermediate principles with
whose help order can be brought into Christian morality. These
principles, it is hoped, will help us descend in an orderly fashion
from general description of the Christian temper to more particular
moral judgments about day-to-day moral questions.

In the past both Catholics and Protestants have introduced at this
point some idea of rules emanating from God – laws or commands.
God has been pictured as like a sovereign who promulgates a body
of positive law. Admittedly his subjects are still left to interpret them,
to work out the casuistry. But the body of divine laws at least gives
them something to work with.

However, this image has many snags. The mere issuing of a
command cannot of itself create a moral duty to obey it. There is
endless disagreement as to how precisely we can discover what God's
commands are, and where they are to be found written down. The
notion of God as a sovereign legislator is an highly anthropomorphic
one, and of course the problems of casuistry are acute. I recently set
a group of young clergymen, as an exercise at a conference, the task
of doing the casuistry for the commandment 'Thou shalt do no
murder', and the results were very various indeed. And finally, a
good deal of what is most important in morality is obviously – when

one thinks of it – not expressible in terms of obedience to rules at all.

The most comprehensive attempt to work out a systematic moral theology is that made in the Catholic Church since the Reformation. It was an attempt to define the minimum standards of conduct permissible in a Christian, devised with the individual in mind, and with a view to being enforced in the confessional. Its structure was thoroughly Aristotelian. It is so often reviled today that many people have forgotten what they are reviling, but in its way it was probably more coherent than anything which has succeeded it.

It was generally set out in three parts: Principles, Precepts and Sacraments. The last of these was something of a curiosity. It was probably present only because textbooks of moral theology were mainly studied by priests, who had charge of the administration of the sacraments and would therefore need to know the regulations connected with them, and the bearing of various points of moral theology upon them. The section on Precepts was rather a muddle. Things to be done and things forbidden were classified in terms of the seven virtues and the alleged seven capital sins – an unhappy classification altogether. The section on Principles was much the clearest and most valuable of the three. It went like this:

Every being has an end, a *telos*. A man is a rational being, who realizes his end in himself by his acts. Moral theology is the practical science of the attainment of the end of man. Thus a treatise of man's last end began the Principles. It has several dimensions: objective and subjective, temporal and eternal, individual and social. (It is a caricature to regard traditional Christian asceticism as oriented solely towards the individual's subjective eternal end. There is more to it than that.) Now the acts through which a man can attain his end are performed in accordance with moral principles directing him to it. Objectively these principles are called law. Their subjective appropriation and application is the work of conscience – that is, the mind's power to frame moral judgments.

This analysis supplies the topics of the various treatises in the volume on Principles. After the dogmatic treatise of man's last end, there follows an account of what a human act is, and of the degrees of knowledge and choice. Then there is an analysis of how the morality of acts is objectively determined and how it may be empirically assessed. Then there are accounts of law, the objective norm of right action, and of conscience, its subjective norm. The various sorts of law are defined – natural, civil, positive, divine and ecclesiastical. And there is of necessity considerable discussion of the uncertainties of conscience, and how a doubtful conscience may be made sure.

It would take a long time to give a just appraisal of the traditional moral theology. Suffice it to say that the criticisms which have been made of it are telling. The structure of the treatises, laboriously built up over centuries, has become like a coral reef, with successive accretions. Drastic reordering is necessary. They are written upon the supposition that the moral life can be dealt with one soul at a time, even one act at a time. They presuppose the truth of a developed dogmatic theology and the *magisterium* of the church in a way that is foreign to most of us nowadays. In times of rapid social change the code soon becomes obsolete and seems comical. The Aristotelian psychology creaks now. And finally, there is the old Socratic theme that virtue is a unity. Any systematic analysis of the moral life is open to the accusation that it is losing sight of the primacy of love, of spontaneity, of the Spirit.

But are those who have criticized the old moral theology bold enough to try to devise an alternative scheme? Hesitantly, I venture below a few suggestions.

In the first place it is no longer so important to distinguish moral theology (the minimum standard required by the church) from Christian ethics (the delineation of the ideal form of Christian life). The institutional aspect of Christianity has long been in decline anyway. Who cares about canon law nowadays?

The old distinction between the natural moral law and positive divine law might be redrawn. P. F. Strawson talks about community rule and personal ideal.[9] G. R. Grice distinguishes 'basic obligations' from 'ultra obligations'.[10] Both roughly distinguish between two areas in morality. First, in any society at any one time there obtains a system of generally binding moral principles, many of them enforced by law, which collectively define what that society regards as the minimum conditions of a tolerable social life. A system of 'basic obligations' is thus created, in which duties correspond to rights. But this schema, certainly in our liberal democracies, is very loose; it supplies a broad social framework, but there is a large second area in morality, of particular interest to novelists, where we are exploring with what content of personal ideals and feelings each individual shall invest his life in society. A man whose morality, however sincere, consisted solely of generally binding moral principles is hardly imaginable.

Here, then, is a way of looking at the traditional distinction between the realms of justice and love, of natural morality and supernatural morality.

But what might be the structure of distinctively Christian moral reasoning? What decides the sort of content a Christian puts into his social life?

Strawson, who is a humanist, sees the formation of the individual's ideal form or forms of life in aesthetic terms. The Christian will see it rather more in theological terms and therefore hopes to bring some rational order into the individual's moral formation. But where does he find his guiding principles?

The principles by reference to which a Christian develops his morality can only be sought in what he makes of the Christian tradition as a whole. But the tradition is notoriously capable of various interpretations. So some guidelines are needed. Any attempt to express these must bear the marks of the period in which it is made. But it may be none the worse for that.

Here are seven principles, stated in as undogmatic a form as possible, with comments where necessary. Without a great deal more reflection I do not know how much to claim for them. But let us be bold and suggest that they are a possible set of guiding principles for Christian moral reasoning which are theologically cautious. If the reader dislikes them, let him take pencil and paper and do better.

1. *The God-relation is not measurable.* What anyone of us is before God is not known to us. That is to say, the most important things about a man are mysterious to us. This seems to me the basis of respect for and restraint in our dealings with people. They are to be regarded as immortal souls.

2. *In the God-relation we are equal.* The notion of moral equality is very slippery, but we can use it without ambiguity in certain contexts. For example, we can speak of the impartiality of the law, and of equal rights safeguarded by law. Theistic morality sees divine justice and love as all-pervading in their impartiality and generosity. If each man is equally important to God, it seems to follow that men should grant each other equal access to the means of having and leading a morally good life. The direction of Christian morality is in the end strongly egalitarian, though any crude dogmatism about this is checked by (1) above.

3. *Covenant.* Men are social beings, and each of us is constituted human by what others have been and are to us. A religious moralist must, I think, reject pictures of mankind as an aggregate of warring individuals each striving to assert himself at the expense of others. He may admire and learn from such as Hobbes or Sartre, but he must say that in the end they are wrong at the crucial point. Love is more 'natural' to us than war.

4. *The goodness of the created order.* This is part of any sort of ethical theism.

5. *A sense of sin.* This is particularly treacherous in that mis-interpretations of it are so productive of evil consequences. If it is used to suggest that 'deep down we are vile' or that children are born wicked it is plainly incompatible with (4). The classical Christian account of evil was of course careful to insist that evil was a contingent and secondary corruption of something in itself good, and something which remained reparable. The traditional stress upon the inwardness of sin had the function of acting as a brake upon rash optimism about human motives and possibilities; it inculcated a sense of limitation, a certain caution. It drew attention to the frightful possibilities for evil in the human heart, and to our need of grace. There is something true and important here, but this particular card is the hardest in the pack to play at the right time, in the right way.

6. *Individuals, and groups, must be willing to go as far as is practically possible in following the methods of love, freedom and persuasion rather than the methods of coercion and the inculcation of fear.* I take this to be the moral conclusion from the life and teaching of Jesus, and that a Christian should be willing to persist with these methods a good deal further than the world thinks wise.

7. *Patterns of imitation and response*, already discussed.

I hope that these seven principles hang together fairly well, and that they succeed both in being reasonably consonant with Christian theism and also in suggesting the broad outlines of a concrete moral policy. It will be noticed that several of them refer back to the realm of social-rule morality, and suggest the interest Christian moralists have in its progressive modification. So, by way of flying a kite, I offer them as one attempt to free Christian moral reasoning of the charge of arbitrariness. The links between religious beliefs and moral policies can only, I think, be rather loose and informal. But that doesn't matter very much.

# 9

## Imitation of God and Imitation of Christ

### BARNABAS LINDARS, SSF

This paper arises directly from the discussion on the paper by Don Cupitt on 'God and Morality' (ch. 8 above), and will be confined to the issue there raised. In that paper it is argued that Christian conduct may be related to Christian doctrine about God, either by making the imitation of God the basis of ethics, or by the concept of response to God in the ways suggested by the imagery we use to think of him. Doubts are expressed about the value of the first alternative, but it is held on the authority of E. J. Tinsley[1] to be an irreducible element of biblical ethics, both in the Old Testament and in the New. In the discussion the question was asked, 'What difference does the Incarnation make to the religious idea of the imitation of God?' The question does not admit of a simple answer, because the imitation of Christ is not necessarily continuous with the imitation of God, extending it and completing it. If the alternative premiss of response to God is preferred, the imitation of Christ may be the use of the traditions about Jesus as the model for response to God. Christ is then the focus for the religious man's striving to make a true response to God. On the other hand, if the basis of Christian ethics is taken to be imitation of God, in whom all morally desirable qualities consist, the Incarnation must be taken to imply the revelation of a quality or qualities hitherto unrecognized, which now become the most important element in moral endeavour.

The difficulty about this view is that the Incarnation cannot be reduced to a quality in God for men to copy. It is, of course, true that the Christ-event tells us something about God, provided that the concept is taken to include the conclusion of that event in the death and resurrection of Jesus. We can then say, 'God loves like that!' This, then, is the model for Christian love, the fundamental disposition of *agape*. But Jesus himself was not a passive agent. The event consisted in a nexus of circumstances, in which he retained moral control against heavy odds because of his unswerving loyalty and obedience to God. But this aspect of the matter places the issue once more in the category of response. The obedience of Christ, so beautifully delineated in the fourth gospel, is an irreducible element of the Christ-event. But, at any rate on a strictly monotheistic view, obedience *to* God cannot be a quality *of* God. It thus becomes necessary to do what was in fact done in the classic formulations of trinitarian doctrine, and take the ethics of response to God into the concept of the inner relations of God as Trinity. Hence the moral impact of the doctrine of the Incarnation is subtly altered. Instead of being the revelation of God's love *for men* as the paradigm for human conduct, it becomes the revelation of a divine society so complete in itself that the love of God for men, however staggering in itself, is a kind of side-show. And this leads to exactly the kind of unsatisfactory ideals which Don Cupitt has pointed out in his paper, e.g. the life of pure contemplation is considered more morally desirable than the life of service to mankind.

It will now be evident that I feel far from satisfied with the idea of imitation of God as a guide to Christian ethics. But my dissatisfaction is not only due to the inherent dangers and difficulties of this idea. As a student of the Bible I feel that it is neither biblical nor true to the ethical position of Jesus and the early church, in so far as these can be recovered from the New Testament. The remainder of this paper will thus be largely a reply to the thesis of Tinsley.[2] But I hope that in the course of it the important theme of the imitation of Christ may be rescued from its involvement with that of the imitation of God and restored to its proper place in New Testament ethics.

When we think of the Old Testament, the most obvious expression of the relation of God and morality is the requirement of obedience to a divinely sanctioned law. But man is not merely God's slave, meekly submitting with unquestioning obedience. He has enough independence of spirit to ask himself why such laws should be necessary. It is the answer to this question which really reveals the ethical relation of man to God. Moreover, it is not only Job who poses this question, nor does the Old Testament give a single consistent answer. There are various answers at different periods of

Israel's history. These are related to the various ways in which men thought of God in different times and circumstances. In so far as there is an unchanging element in the Israelite idea of God, the notion of ethical relation remains constant in spite of differing emphases.

It is a commonplace of study that in the ancient world the way in which the gods are pictured is to some extent a reflection of the social conditions of those who worship them. The Old Testament does not present a single sociological picture, but a complex development. This is reflected in the varying attitudes to God and morality, and it is essential to assess correctly their relative importance.

(*a*) The period of the patriarchal narratives in Genesis and of the exodus and conquest, when critically examined, shows Israel as a semi-nomadic society. As this period, strictly speaking, belongs to prehistoric times, and as all the documentation derives from a later period after the settlement, it was formerly regarded as too unreliable to produce any firm conclusions. But it has received a flood of light from the comparative material of the contemporary texts from Mari and Nuzi, which show that the ancient traditions retain a remarkably accurate picture of sociological conditions.[3] The dominant factor in such a society is the necessity of maintaining the kinship-group, in order to preserve tribal identity. It is a patriarchal society. The tribe worships the god of their father, who is himself thought of in patriarchal terms (hence the theophoric names compounded with *'ab* = father, e.g. Abram, Abraham, Abimelech). This implies virtual monotheism, at least within the kinship-group. Just as mutual trust and loyalty to the group are essential to the tribe's survival, so God is loyal to the people who are akin to him. Each kinship-group is vigorously independent. The code of behaviour towards men of another tribe is dictated by the attitude of the whole tribe, varying from active hostility to close co-operation. The latter usually implies the recognition of some degree of consanguinity.

The moral attributes of God correspond with the essential ethical needs of life of the semi-nomadic pattern. Foremost among these are two of the most enduring qualities in the biblical idea of God, *ḥesed we'ᵉmeth*. The phrase is translated 'mercy and truth' in Ex. 34.6 (*RV*), but the real meaning of these words is loyalty to the group and steadfast reliability. It is these qualities (reinterpreted in the light of later ideas) which are displayed by God in the revelation of himself at the Incarnation according to the fourth gospel ('full of grace and truth', John 1.14, probably based on Ex. 34.6). The point of this observation is that these are not primarily virtues to imitate, but indispensable conditions of existence. They are necessary constituents of the relationship between man and God, just as they are between man and man. They are required on both sides. God's *ḥesed weʾemeth* are held up as an example simply because God, being so much greater than men, evinces them in an exemplary manner. But the ground of the ethical relationship is not imitation, but the fact of belonging together in a group.

(*b*) The settlement in Canaan brought Israel into contact with the cultic pattern of the Fertile Crescent. This brings into play a totally different idea of man's ethical relation to God. Of course, the Canaanite cities did not present anything approaching the highly organized society of the great alluvial regions of the Nile Delta and Lower Mesopotamia. But the pattern of life was equally tied to the soil. Seed-time and harvest dictated the rhythm of life, which in other respects was static. The basis of society was not ethnic, except in so far as social stratification reflected the subjugation of successive ethnic groups. But it was rather the concept of ownership which determined the behaviour-patterns of these settled peoples. The slaves and lower classes were subject to the upper classes, so that there was a pyramidical structure with the king at the apex. The gods constituted a divine society comparable to the royal court.[4] The high god, often identified with the sun, held the place of the king. How far the earthly king was considered to be divine is disputable. Even if he is described as God's son by adoption (cf. Ps. 2.7), his relation to God is one of subordination to the true owner of the land. Besides the obvious need to maintain the *status quo* in such a society, the paramount requirement was the fertility of the soil. The gods are to some extent weather-gods, but the mystery of life involves something more than winter rains and the inundation of river valleys. The agrarian peoples felt that there was an intimate connection between sexual potency and the fertility of the land. The well-being of the land was inextricably involved in the life-and-death struggles of the gods. It can scarcely be expected in such a situation that the imitation of God will provide a basis for moral life. Imitation is an important element in the fertility rituals, embodying the dramatic representation of the myths, but this is mainly a matter of sympathetic magic, in order to secure control over the supernatural powers. But even this is dictated by the idea of ownership, as the people are bound to perform these acts in order to satisfy the arbitrary requirements of their divine overlords.

The institution of the monarchy in Israel was bound to bring with it some measure of these attitudes at the highest level, in addition to the widespread popular assimilation of Canaanite ways. But it is the attempt of Jezebel in the ninth century BC to make the worship of Baal Melkart the official religion of Israel, which reveals most clearly the ethical consequences. Just as in the Ugaritic texts Baal ousted the old high god El from his supremacy, so Jezebel was determined to bring her husband's realm under the lordship of her own god. Under her influence Ahab claims the right of an absolute monarch, and sets aside the Israelite laws of inheritance in order to secure for his own use Naboth's vineyard. It is no accident that the same word *ba'al* is the name (or title) of the god who claims ownership of the land, is commonly used of a husband in a society where women had no rights, and is also used of the owner of a slave.

Although the work of the prophets ensured the survival of the fundamental nomadic ideas of God and morality, which were taken up into the great reform of Israel's religion during and after the Babylonian exile, the Canaanite ideas left their mark. God had acquired the characteristics of the high god, and was thought of in terms of royalty. In the post-exilic period he is the Great King. It is at this point that obedience to the law becomes the most characteristic way of understanding the ethical relation of God and man. But God's claim upon the people's obedience rests upon a new concept, that of the election of Israel. The notion is not new in one sense. It is really the nomadic idea of belonging together in a group. But instead of basing this on kinship, it puts it in the form of God's free choice of a people for himself. This goes far back into history, as the moment of choice is identified as the exodus from Egypt. It is thus directly related to the central cultic tradition peculiar to Israel. As a matter of history, it is probably true to say that Yahweh's choice of Israel was really Israel's choice of Yahweh, when he was identified as their deliverer from the bondage of Egypt. The idea allowed the ethical relationship of the nomadic kinship pattern to exist, in spite of the fact that Yahweh was not really the God of the Fathers (though of course he was formally identified with him). This became an important factor when non-Israelite elements were absorbed into the Yahwistic community during the period of conquest.

The Sinai covenant, which has received very great attention in recent study, is obviously relevant here. My excuse for not mentioning it before is that I think that the covenant created the conditions for the semi-nomadic pattern to predominate in the conquest period, but that it did not of itself form the basis of Israelite ethics. There was nothing contractual about Israel's relation to God. The election of Israel gives the sense of belonging to Yahweh as his people, without the Canaanite notion of ownership. The idea is first used in an ethical sense by Amos, 'You only have I known of all the families of the earth; therefore I will punish you for your iniquities' (Amos 3.2). However, it receives its greatest impetus from the work of the Deuteronomic reformers, who stress God's special love for Israel on the basis of the exodus tradition. This continues in the post-exilic religious ethics, and compensates for the growing tendency to place the emphasis on the transcendence of God. It was incorporated into a universalistic frame of thought by means of the Wisdom tradition (see especially Ecclus. 24).

(*c*) One other ground of ethical thought must be mentioned, which is common to both the nomadic and Canaanite patterns, and that is the distinction between sacred and profane. In the Canaanite setting this is connected, as we should expect, with places and things and cultic persons. But the idea of the 'tent of meeting' is probably to be traced back to a similar phenomenon in semi-nomadic society. And, of course, places where God has manifested himself are regarded as his home (e.g. Sinai). The idea is not necessarily ethical, and indeed tends to lead to inextricable confusion between moral and ceremonial requirements. But it certainly exercised an immense influence over patterns of behaviour in the ancient world, as it does to this day.

It is clear that in the long history of Israelite thought there was considerable interaction of these fundamental ideas. One notable consequence is the way in which Isaiah invests the notion of holiness, inherent in the pattern of sacral kingship derived from Canaan, with a profoundly ethical tone. The preoccupation with maintaining the purity, characteristic of pharisaic and rabbinic Judaism, shows how the primitive feelings of holiness and uncleanness can become transformed by the concept of obedience to divine law, thus perpetuating the confusion between ethical and non-ethical requirements at the same time as bringing all under one ethical motive.

We are now in a position to look afresh at the ways in which it is alleged that the imitation of God is a factor in biblical ethics. In the first place there is the imitation of the divine attributes. We have already dealt with this in relation to the virtues of *ḥesed* and *'ᵉmeth*. These are not held up as something to be copied, but are recognized to be fundamental conditions for the existence of personal relationships within the group, whether beween man and man or man and God. But the idea of imitation seems to be present on two occasions when David undertakes to do 'the *ḥesed* of the Lord' (I Sam. 20.14) or 'of God' (II Sam. 9.3) in his dealing with the royal house of Saul. One may well think of this as magnanimity on the divine scale. But it seems to me more likely that it refers to David's deeply felt concern for the due fulfilment of his oath of allegiance to the house of Saul, which remained operative (or would remain operative in the first instance) even when he himself became king. The second case has been interpreted as a superlative expression,[5] but this seems to me to be doubtful.

It is often asserted that justice in Israel is inculcated on the basis of God's righteousness, though this has to be deduced from the texts, for it is not explicitly stated. It is really another case of what has just been said about the other two attributes. There is, however, an additional complication in that the administration of justice is a divine activity performed by men as God's delegates. Their decisions must be just and impartial, not just in imitation of God, but because they are his decisions, or rather the application of his law. The earliest law codes are cast in the form of the words of God, his stipulations which are laid upon the people when they are brought into the Israelite kinship-group by covenant in the sense outlined above. Even the king is subject to God's law; see the test case of Naboth's vineyard, I Kings 21.

On the other hand, we do get a direct exhortation to imitate God in the watchword of the Holiness Code (Lev. 17–26): 'Be ye holy, for I am holy.' But the words must be seen in their context to be properly understood. This code is a collection of moral and cultic laws, probably compiled in connection with an effort for reform. An attempt has been made to bring the disparate material under a single heading by the repeated slogan, 'I am the Lord'. The various laws are not advanced for ethical or humanitarian reasons, but because they are God's own commands. All the laws are aimed at maintaining holiness and removing impurity, i.e. they are considered from the point of view of the special expertise of the priests. God himself, of course, belongs to the sphere of the holy. If the people are to belong to him, they must be holy too (Lev. 20.26). What has happened is that the old idea of belonging together with God in a group has now taken on the idea of holiness as the necessary condition for preserving identity, instead of loyalty, etc. This might be written off as the triumph of impersonal and mechanical views, if it were not for the fact that the idea of God's holiness had already acquired an ethical tone. The command is not to imitate God's holiness, but to *be* holy *because* he is holy. Otherwise Israel cannot belong to the same group.

It is in the Deuteronomic literature that the idea of mimesis is most marked. This is certainly due to its strongly didactic aim and method. Tinsley stresses the correlation between the 'way' of the wanderings in the desert and the 'way' of personal conduct. The hortatory sections of Deuteronomy go over all the main incidents of the desert wanderings from this point of view. Naturally the people's failings are held up as a warning, and God's saving mercies are held up for emulation. It is simply an application of the familiar teaching-method of the use of historical characters for moral example. But the chief character happens to be God. This is not fortuitous, because the area of history chosen for such examples is the saving history, and this is precisely because it gives the grounds for God's claims on the people's allegiance (cf. the remarks above on election). But for the purposes of ethical instruction this history remains illustrative. It does not provide a programme of ethics, nor does it recommend the imitation of God as a solution to the problems of decision-making. It is presupposed that these will be solved by reference to the actual laws.

In the same way we must be wary of reading too much into Deuteronomic explanations of laws in terms of mimesis. These are added to reinforce the moral sanction of a law which can be neglected with impunity. The appeal to God's mercy in the saving history is aimed at arousing religious emotions, so as to persuade people to be more conscientious in keeping a law or a precept with which they are already thoroughly familiar. An obvious case is the law of manumission of slaves (compare Ex. 21.2–6 with Deut. 15.12–18). The law of the sabbath is particularly instructive. This is one of the Ten Commandments which has obviously undergone expansion at various times. In Deut. 5.15 the point is pressed home that even slaves are to enjoy the benefit of it, and the slavery of the Israelites in Egypt is adduced. But in Ex. 20.11 this is missing, and instead

there is a possibly post-deuteronomic addition explaining the institution of the sabbath by reference to the creation story. This may
well reflect the importance of the sabbath during the exile, when it
became one of the 'Noachic precepts'.

It is really not until New Testament times that the imitation of
God becomes a factor in Jewish ethical thought. Even then it remains
peripheral. Philo is certainly indebted to Greek speculative thought
in using this idea. But his work stands right outside the main Jewish
traditions. Tinsley quotes from Israel Abrahams Jewish interpretations of scripture which built on the idea of becoming like God. But
this is not the same thing as the imitation of God as a basis of ethics.

In dealing with the New Testament it is clearly necessary to
observe a careful distinction between imitation of God and imitation
of Christ. The latter is undoubtedly a most important theme in early
Christianity. It appears both in the teaching of Jesus himself and in
the teaching of Paul. But it only takes a little familiarity with the
texts to realize that this is the common rabbinic notion of mimesis
as a quality of discipleship. The Master lives out the ethic which he
teaches, and the disciple learns as much by imitation as by listening.
This appears most clearly in the theme of martyrdom, reflected in
the sayings about taking up one's cross. Such references show Jesus
not only as the Master, whose lead is to be followed, but also as
himself the model disciple. The famous christological hymn in
Phil. 2.5-11 is used in this way. The idea of Jesus as the model
disciple is also very prominent in the fourth gospel, where Jesus'
relation to the Father is expressed in terms of filial obedience and
held up to the disciples to copy.

The Deuteronomic idea of the saving history as a pattern for
ethics continued to some extent in Judaism, and reappears in the
New Testament. From the point of view of soteriology the events
of the death and resurrection of Christ fulfil the Old Testament
types. As the same pattern is reproduced in the life of the Christian,
who appropriates salvation through baptism into Christ's death, it is
tempting to correlate imitation of Christ by the Christian with
Christ's own imitation of God. But such an idea betrays confusion
of thought. Soteriology and ethics are not the same thing. The ethical
consequences of redemption do not consist in imitation but in
response to what has been achieved. Paul uses the salvation history
for moral example, notably in I Cor. 10, exactly in the same way as
it is used in Deuteronomy.[6] How far Jesus himself deliberately

reproduced this history in his own ministry is a very debatable point. I cannot accept Tinsley's claim that 'Jesus willed to mime the significant features of his nation's history' (p. 72). The signs done by Jesus show that the kingdom of God is at hand, but they are not mimesis of God in an ethical sense. In fact the whole burden of Jesus' ethical teaching is to put in the most uncompromising way the challenge to behaviour involved in confrontation with the *Deus praesens*. And this does not take the form of imitating God, but of existential demand. It is, then, an ethic of response.

But the imitation of God is not wholly absent from the teaching of Jesus, and it is important that we should understand its scope. The most obvious example is Matt. 5.48: 'Be ye therefore perfect, even as your Father which is in heaven is perfect' (*AV*). Tinsley rightly notes that this is a variant of Luke 6.36, and is to be interpreted by it: 'Be ye therefore merciful, as your Father also is merciful' (*AV*). For the two words in Hebraic thought both refer to integrity (or loyalty) of behaviour. The saying leads us back to the *ḥesed we'emeth*, which are essential to both sides in the God-man relationship, and are pre-eminently exemplified by God on his side. It is, then, an exhortation to men to keep their side of the same obligation. To this extent men's behaviour is modelled on God's, because God's behaviour is precisely what man's should be. It is not a case of contemplation of divine perfections, which are then put into practical form in an ethical context. It is rather that God's goodness recalls men to consider responsibly their own goodness.

On the other hand there are certain ways in which God's ethics *differ* from those required of men. The parable of the labourers in the vineyard depends upon this very fact. Men are also warned not to judge one another, as if they were taking the part of God. This thought has its counterpart in I Peter 1.17, where the writer warns his readers not to suppose that the fatherhood of God makes him any less strict and impartial as their Judge. In the same context 'Be ye holy, for I am holy' is quoted, and expressly interpreted in terms of mimesis. But the larger context is that of the transition from the old life to the new effected in baptism, so that the quotation retains its proper connotation of transference to the sphere of the sacred.

If we would be true to biblical ethics, we would do well to treat the notion of imitation of God with some reserve. It is only valid as a facet of the alternative ethic of response, i.e. that to believe *that* God characteristically acts in a loving way is to be disposed to do so oneself. The position of Jesus himself is that of response, and the concept of the imitation of Christ only comes in, even within the teaching of Jesus himself, on account of the pupil-teacher relationship, as the means of reproducing that response in his followers. The Incarnation does not warrant an attempt to lift the ethics of God's way with men into the essential being of God apart from men. This can only be done by way of analogy, and we cannot jump straight back from there to the morality of men.

# 10

# Protestant Ethics and the Will of God

## JAMES WHYTE

'It cannot be nor need it be denied that men who seriously ask, as
religious men, what they are to do know that the answer is "the
will of God".'[1]

I suppose that this is a characteristically Protestant statement; not
that other Christians would deny that a religious man is called to do
God's will, but that this formulation of the ethical answer is an
emphasis characteristic both of Protestant piety and of Protestant
theology. The purpose of this paper is to consider whether this
emphasis has been a helpful one; whether it has value today; and
whether, when one faces the consequent questions (e.g. how do I
know the will of God?) this approach is found to have any advantages over others.

### I

The idea of the will of God as an ethical norm goes back into the
roots of Protestant thought in the nominalist philosophy. The ethical
aspect of nominalism is voluntarism, in which the answer to the old
riddle 'Is a thing good because God wills it, or does God will it
because it is good?' is given unequivocally in terms of the former
alternative. As nominalism leads in theology to a dependence on
revelation (God is known only as he wills to reveal himself in scripture), so in ethics it leads to a dependence on the revealed will of
God. Indeed, it can be said that all that is known of God is his will;
his dealings with men are revealed in the *voluntas beneplaciti*, his
commands for men in the *voluntas signi*.

This is found with particular force in the thought of Calvin and
of Calvinism. God orders all things according to the will of his good

pleasure. There can be no arguing with this sovereign will, and no accusation against God of injustice. If, in his inscrutable will, he has from all eternity predestined some men and angels to eternal life and others to eternal damnation, man has no right to bring his human ideas of justice forward in complaint against this. Calvin answers those who object to the injustice of the doctrine of double predestination by asking them to consider

how exceedingly presumptuous it is only to inquire into the causes of the Divine will; which is in fact, and is justly entitled to be, the cause of every thing that exists. For if it has any cause, then there must be something antecedent, on which it depends; which it is impious to suppose. For the will of God is the highest rule of justice; so that what he wills must be considered just, for this very reason, because he wills it. When it is inquired, therefore, why the Lord did so, the answer must be, Because he would. But if you go further, and ask why he so determined, you are in search of something greater and higher than the will of God, which can never be found.[2]

God's will for man, his rule, is expressed in the law. This has not only (as for Luther) the uses of restraining sin in the world, and bringing the sinner to repentance, but for Calvin has also a third and principal use, for Christians.

For they find it an excellent instrument to give them from day to day a better and more certain understanding of the Divine will to which they aspire, and to confirm them in the knowledge of it.[3]

Calvin gives a lengthy exposition of the decalogue as the sum of the moral law, but when he comes later to give an account of the Christian life he does not pick up again his exposition of the Ten Commandments.

Although the Divine law contains a most excellent and well-arranged plan for the regulation of life, yet it has pleased the heavenly Teacher to conform men by a more accurate doctrine to the rule which he has prescribed in the law. And the principle of that doctrine is this; that it is the duty of the faithful to 'present their bodies a living sacrifice, holy, acceptable unto God;' and that in this consists the legitimate worship of him. Hence is deduced an argument for exhorting them; 'Be not conformed to this world: but be ye transformed by the renewing of your mind, that ye may prove what is the will of God.'[4]

This is the life of self-denial, of devotion to God and to the neighbour.

Indeed, a Christian man ought to be so composed and prepared, as to reflect that he has to do with God every moment of his life. Thus, as he will measure all his actions by His will and determination, so he will refer the whole bias of his mind religiously to Him.[5]

There are two ways in which an ethic based on the will of God can operate, and both tendencies are found in Calvinism. It can become a legalism, which takes the law of God as the revealed rule by which alone we can know his will; or a personalism, which sees the law only as one form and that not the most accurate (to use Calvin's term) by which a personal divine will presses upon us in every moment of our life. It may be an ethic of the divine command-ments, or an ethic of the divine command.

These two tendencies are present but not explicitly distinguished in Calvin himself; and the Calvinist scholastics of the seventeenth century were content for the most part with a legalistic interpretation of the divine will. In the modern revival of Reformed theology, how-ever, the other alternative has been dominant. Both Barth and Brunner speak in voluntarist terms. For Brunner, 'The Good is simply and solely the will of God';[6] 'What God does and wills is good; all that opposes the will of God is bad. The Good has its basis and its existence solely in the will of God.'[7] This is Brunner's inter-pretation of the Old Testament message, which, he holds, is equally true of the Christian message. Barth, similarly, can speak of 'the reality of the command of God as the sum of the good'.[8] For Barth this reality is the reality of God's grace, and this command is at the same time a gift – the gift of freedom. For Brunner, the Divine Imperative is also both gift and demand.

In faith God claims us for His will. . . . We *may* believe, we *can* believe – this is God's word of grace; we *ought* to believe – this is His Com-mand. . . . The Law, so far as its content is concerned, is severed from the grace of God; the Command, however, can only be understood as the address of the gracious and generous God who claims me for Himself the gracious Giver, that I may *belong* to Him. Hence I cannot know beforehand the content of the Command as I can know that of the Law; I can only receive it afresh each time through the voice of the Spirit.[9]

For Barth,

The question of good and evil is never answered by man's pointing to the authoritative Word of God in terms of a set of rules. It is never dis-covered by man or imposed on the self and others as a code of good and evil actions, a sort of yardstick of what is good and evil. Holy Scripture defies being forced into a set of rules; it is a mistake to use it as such. The ethicist cannot take the place either of the free God or of free man, even less of both together.[10]

The lawgiver, as Barth says, does not retreat behind his law.

Thus the tendency in this century has been to interpret an ethic of the will of God in strongly anti-legalistic terms. 'Legalism is always the worst kind of corruption.'[11] In an early writing (1929) of Dietrich Bonhoeffer this seems to have become quite antinomian.

For the Christian there are no ethical principles by means of which he could perhaps civilize himself. Nor can yesterday ever be decisive for my moral action today. Rather must a direct relationship to God's will be ever sought afresh. I do not do something again today because it seemed to me to be good yesterday, but because the will of God points out this way to me today. . . . For the Christian there is no other law than the law of freedom, as the New Testament paradoxically puts it. No generally valid law which could be expounded to him by others, or even by himself. The man who surrenders freedom surrenders his very nature as a Christian. The Christian stands free, without any protection, before God and before the world, and he alone is wholly responsible for what he does with the gift of freedom. Now through this freedom the Christian becomes creative in ethical action. Acting in accordance with principles is unproductive, imitating the law, copying. Acting from freedom is creative. . . . Time-honoured morals – even if they are given out to be the consensus of Christian opinion – can never for the Christian become the standard of his actions. He acts, because the will of God seems to bid him to. . . . Now, day by day, hour by hour, we are confronted with unparalleled situations in which we must make a decision, and in which we must make again and again the surprising and terrifying discovery that the will of God does not reveal itself before our eyes as clearly as we had hoped. . . . The decision which is freely required must be made freely by each person in the concrete situation. . . .[12]

## II

I do not intend to embark on any detailed criticism of the writers I have quoted extensively above; they have been chosen as representing a tendency, and the differences between them have been ignored. But I wish to look at some of the objections that can be raised against the interpretation of morality in terms of the will of God.

(i) The voluntarist answer to the old dilemma of whether a thing is *ius quia iustum* or *ius quia iussum* (right because it is just or because it is commanded)[13] is open to obvious objections, since it appears to make God's will arbitrary, and leaves us dependent entirely upon authority for our moral guidance. No kind of insight is possible; we must simply do as we are told. On this view, if God's will were to change from day to day, man would still be bound to obey. If God commanded murder, instead of forbidding it, then man's righteousness would consist in murder. This makes it possible to accept without moral difficulties such a conception as the *ḥerem* in the Old Testament, by which the Israelites believed themselves commanded by God to commit genocide.[14] It also makes it easy – or unnecessary – to justify the ways of God to man, as these are disclosed in the divine decrees, and the doctrine of double predestination. (Paul seems to make use of this kind of argument in Rom. 9.14–21.)

But we cannot rest content with a view which reduces the divine right to arbitrary power. In fact, when Calvin leaves the subject of the Divine decrees, he always speaks of the righteousness of God in terms that clearly indicate a moral reality – i.e. something more than bare *will*. The eighteenth-century Calvinist scholar, Petrus van Mastricht, posing the question 'whether a thing is righteous because God wills it to be righteous, or on the other hand God wills it because it is right', distinguishes between God's will and his nature.

Certain things we conceive to be righteous antecedently to God's will, although they are not so antecedently to his nature. . . . Some things are righteous just because God wills them, i.e. those which are *iuris positivi*. Some things God wills because they are righteous, those which are *iuris naturalis*, so far as they agree with the holiness of his nature, or with the nature of man, so far as he bears the image of God.[15]

Mastricht thus avoids being impaled on the other horn of the dilemma, because to say that God wills a thing because it is righteous is not necessarily to imply the existence of a rule, higher and greater than God himself, to which he is subject; the rule is his own nature. This means, however, that he has abandoned the strict nominalist position, and accepts that we can have not only authoritative revelation about God's will, but also some knowledge of his nature. This means further that the authority of a command derives not simply from its purporting to come from God, but rather from its being seen to be in accordance with his nature. Karl Barth is quite explicit on this point. The authority of the divine claim derives from its graciousness.[16]

If one meant by 'God' simply 'the supreme ruler of the universe', then Professor Nowell-Smith's contention would be justified, viz. that the fact that a command has been given by God is not a logically good reason for obeying it.[17] If it could be shown that the supreme ruler of the universe was a cruel and degrading tyrant, then it would be better to die defying his commands than to live as his servant.[18] 'Shall not the judge of all the earth do right?' is a reasonable claim made by man upon God. We do not mean by 'God' simply 'the supreme ruler of the universe'. Indeed, theologians today are more inclined to re-interpret God's power and rule in the light of what they know and believe about his goodness, than to make his power essential and his goodness an accident. To say that the authority of the divine claim derives from its graciousness, or that his claim upon us can be recognized as a moral claim, is to accept that all talk about God is value-laden.

(ii) H. P. Owen, in his first essay in this series, draws attention to another objection of Professor Nowell-Smith against the interpretation of morality in terms of the will of God, viz. that to regard God as an omnipotent legislator is to adopt an infantile attitude of dependence that is incompatible with moral maturity.

It must be acknowledged that many of those who call themselves Christians have adopted – though I think it would be more accurate to say, are fixed in – an infantile attitude of dependence. A glance at any hymn-book is all that is needed to verify this judgment. There is no doubt that the language of obedience – especially that of un-questioning obedience – to the divine command is very congenial to such an attitude. It may be further conceded that the 'omnipotent legislator' view of God – i.e. the legalistic option in ethics – tends to express this attitude. The biblical legalist is one who finds security in the authoritative and revealed law of God to which he submits. (He does not notice how much of what he claims to be God's revealed will lies in his own interpretation of the scriptures.) The sado-masochistic personality – on the one hand deeply submissive to the divine authority, on the other hand stern and rigorous as an instrument of that authority upon others – is a common enough phenomenon.

But these attitudes are not peculiar to the interpretation of morality in terms of the will of God. All legalistic interpretations of ethics share in this attitude of infantile dependence, and represent a shrinking from moral maturity. Paul certainly seems to have understood legalism in this way (Gal. 3.23–4.7). Further, all authoritarian forms of ethics or religion express this attitude – the authority of the bishop may be for some a nearer and more secure authority than their own interpretation of scripture. And, as I suggested above, it seems much more likely that people adopt a particular point of view in ethics or theology because of the need to satisfy their infantile dependence, than that a particular point of view leads them to adopt an attitude of infantile dependence.

Indeed, as the quotation given above from Bonhoeffer shows, and as the development of this type of ethic into situationism suggests, the interpretation of ethics in terms of God's will is far from incompatible with the claims of freedom and maturity. Indeed, the great problem of this interpretation has been its tendency to throw up spirit-guided and antinomian movements whose confident claims to divine inspiration, or to the right to judge all things, are very far from infantile dependence. The point that emerges from this criticism is rather this: that if ethics is understood in terms of a relationship to God, then everything depends on how that relationship is understood. Submission to a tyrant is one thing; the freedom of an adult son is another.

(iii) The interpretation of ethics in terms of the will of God may, as I have suggested above, be disentangled from the nominalist philosophy; in which case, as Lehmann suggests, it may be almost a cliché to give the answer 'Do the will of God' to the question 'What am I to do?' For while the answer may be true enough, it no longer provides any simple or distinctive ethical norm. The question remains, 'How do I know the will of God?' Once you abandon an exclusive dependence on a revealed law, explicit commandments given in scripture (and that is not such a simple answer as it seems), no simple answer remains. It seems that we are left with the same problem that the ethicist has in determining how one knows what is good or right – and with a similar choice of answers, corresponding roughly to the different schools of moral philosophy. At the opposite end from the view that God's will has been revealed once for all in ten (or more) commandments, is the belief in guidance by the Spirit – the Christian has a hot line to the Almighty, and gets his orders every morning (or more frequently, if required). The will of God may be made known through the teaching tradition of the church, the advice of a pastoral counsellor, the dictates of conscience, the natural law. We may believe, with Joseph Fletcher, that 'The ruling norm of Christian decision is love: nothing else.'[19] We may go further, and say that love of the neighbour means in fact seeking the greatest happiness of the greatest number, thus reversing Mill's proposition that 'To do as you would be done by, and to love your neighbour as yourself, constitute the ideal perfection of utilitarian morality.'[20] We may believe that God's will is revealed in Jesus Christ himself, the Word incarnate. We may believe, with Lehmann, that it is found by discerning what God is doing in the world 'to make and keep human life human'.[21] The fact that this whole range of options is available seems to suggest that no practical advantage derives from this interpretation of Christian morality.

On the contrary, I think that the interpretation of morality in terms of the will of God has this advantage, that none of these norms can be an absolute authority. There may indeed be various sources of *guidance* for the Christian in discerning the will of God, but none of them can claim absolute or final *authority*. There is room for discussion regarding the theological significance and the moral weight to be given to each of them, but none of them, nor any number taken together, can provide a text from which we can read off the answer to the question 'What am I to do?' The best statement of this that I know is that given by J. H. Oldham in the preparatory work for the 1937 Oxford Conference on Church, Community and State. In his section on 'An Ethic of Inspiration' he says, 'The basis of the Christian ethic is faith in a living, personal God who has disclosed His grace and His will in Jesus Christ',[22] and insists 'that the fundamental and characteristic thing in Christian action is not obedience to fixed norms or a moral code, but living response to a Person'.[23] But he is careful to qualify his conception of 'inspiration' in this way.

The view that the spring of Christian action is response to a God who is free and sovereign, who makes known His will in the living present to those who humbly seek to know it, does not involve any arbitrariness or individualism. The God to whom we are called to respond is not capricious but constant in His dealings with men. In each new situation in which men find themselves His will can be learned only in the light of His will already revealed in Christ, in the Bible and in the experience of the Church.[24]

I wonder if there is a parallel here with the Reformed use of creeds and confessions. The Reformed churches make use of a large number of creeds, confessions, catechisms, but none of them – not even the ancient symbols – can claim final authority for faith.

## III

I wish finally to suggest some Christian insights which the interpretation of ethics in terms of the will of God helps to preserve – to put it no higher than that.

(i) There is a clear concern in all modern writers who use these terms to preserve the truth of justification by faith. 'There are countless ways from man to God, and therefore also countless ethics, but there is only one way from God to man, and that is the way of love in Christ, the way of the cross.'[25] The Christian ethic is a response to a gracious and forgiving God; and it is the response of men who by that grace have been given dignity, status and confidence as sons of God. If then morality is thought of as 'doing the will of God', the source of the moral demand is the same God who is to us grace and forgiveness. They need not even be separated, as by Luther, into God's left hand and his right. This means that self-righteousness – which is also self-centredness and unbelief – the effort to establish our virtue, to have something to our credit, an achievement with which to purchase divine favour, or to build up confidence in one's worth, is excluded, because the attitude is simply incompatible with a relationship to a gracious and forgiving God. This unity of moral demand and saving grace may be lost when morality is thought of in terms of abstract standards, laws or values, without reference to a personal divine will.[26] This tendency can be seen in certain developments of Situation Ethics, which issue in a form of utilitarianism, which is designed to enable the agent to feel justified by his works, even when his pursuit of the greatest good of the greatest number involves much evil and suffering for the lesser number. The 'agapeic calculus'[27] replaces the 'living response to a Person'.

(ii) There is a concern to preserve 'the liberty of the Christian man', which Luther saw was the Pauline corollary to justification by faith. 'Freedom' is the refrain in Barth's ethics, though the account he gives of freedom is somewhat unusual. Christian liberty, understood in the light of Paul's letter to the Galatians, must be given its proper place in any interpretation of Christian ethics. Calvin understood Christian liberty as the Christian, whose heart has been touched by God, doing willingly what the law commands. Perhaps the aspect of Christian liberty which most requires to be stressed is that of discernment, the Christian's liberty to judge for himself, 'to discern the will of God, and to know what is good, acceptable and perfect'.[28]

There is ground for suggesting that the Christian answer to the question 'How do I know the will of God?' is 'You come to discern it'. 'Come to', because it is not suggested that this is an immediate and automatic result of Christian faith. The context is that in which Paul speaks of the offering of the self, the worship of heart and mind, in response to God's mercy; and of the renewing of the mind. We may say then that as we respond to the mercy of God which we see in Jesus, our mind is opened through our knowledge of him, and we begin to discern, to see for ourselves, to have some insight into, what is good, acceptable and perfect – what is the will of God. This account of Christian liberty is not only compatible with an ethic of the will of God, but seems to require it.

There seems to be a similarity between moral and aesthetic discernment.[29] Presented with a painting one has never seen before, one may still recognize the work of a particular artist, and say 'That is Matisse – or Chagall – or Davie'. This recognition is a result of acquaintance with these men's work in the past, and it may have been helped by the reading of art criticism, and an analysis of their techniques and style. Nevertheless, the recognition is immediate. It is not itself the result of an analysis. It may, of course, be mistaken; in which case we learn from our mistakes. In a more general way, we come to discern what is good art and to distinguish it from what is meretricious. This again is influenced by education and experience, but it issues in judgments which are immediate, personal and fallible – in times of rapid change, very fallible. Now in some regards moral discernment is not like this, for one is not presented with a finished picture, to ask who painted it, or whether it is good or bad. It is more like learning to see the scene itself with the painter's eye, to discern the patterns, to pick out the significant lines, to know what he would make of it. But it is similar in this, that moral analysis (like conscience itself) deals properly with the past, with what has already been done. It helps to educate moral discernment, but that discernment, when made upon new material, is always immediate and personal, and, however fallible, a kind of 'seeing'.

(iii) It seems that when ethics is grounded in a relationship to a personal and gracious will it will more readily produce an attitude which is open to relationships to others. Brunner describes one of the dangers of legalism.

The legalistic type of person finds it impossible to come into real human, personal contact with his fellow-man. Between him and his neighbour there stands something impersonal, the 'idea', the 'Law', a programme, something abstract which hinders him from seeing the other person as he really is, which prevents him from hearing the real claim which his neighbour makes on him.[30]

Much ethical thinking deals with the individual as isolated, in his will, decision, duty, virtue, as though relationships with other selves were not an essential part of the moral situation. Christian love can be described as disinterested benevolence, involving no personal encounter with any particular neighbour. It seems that in the New Testament, however, 'love' is a relational term, and that the New Testament ethic (especially in the ethical sections of the epistles) is concerned with the qualities, attitudes, actions which make for good human relationships, and the restoration of broken relationships. The grounding of morality in the will of a gracious and forgiving God is, to say the least, conducive to this responsiveness to persons.

(iv) The grounding of ethics in a personal divine will may help in emphasizing the historical character of human life. In all the changing situations of life and of history, one is seeking to discern the will of a God who is present and at work in the world. Even in unprecedented situations, the Christian may discern the divine will. It is argued that Situationism makes too much of the uniqueness of situations, and that in any case this is not what ethics is about. Certainly no situation is unique in the sense of being totally unlike any other situation, but equally no situation is exactly like any other – 'we do not step twice into the same river', as Heraclitus observed. In the rapid advance of scientific technology we are faced with many situations of moral decision which have a strong element of novelty, of the unprecedented. The 'will of God' ethic has the possibility of openness to the changing situation.

(v) The interpretation of ethics in terms of the will of God is concerned to maintain the conviction that in any situation, however unprecedented, or however morally ambiguous, there is one course of action, one choice, which is for us the will of God. If the choice is between two evils, then one of these evils is, in that situation, the will of God, and must be done with a good conscience. Thus Karl Barth stresses 'the particularity of the divine command'. I have suggested, in (i) above, the danger that if this understanding of God's will is separated from his saving grace, it becomes a method of justification by works, of salving one's conscience in the midst of moral compromise, while doing evil that good may come. It may become a way in which one can evade the real confrontation with evil and the tragic dimension in human life. But if the understanding of God's will for us in each situation is held in close connection with his saving grace, as seen in the cross of Christ, it involves the positive belief that no situation is morally hopeless, and the concern, not simply to find a balance of good over evil, but to find the ways in which good can come out of evil. In this way one may speak of 'creative morality', as action which is not imprisoned in the terms in which a situation seems to present itself, but seeks and finds the 'creative edge', the way that is open to new possibilities in the future. This seems more likely to come from those who interpret their ethic in terms of the will of a gracious God than from those who are enclosed in the law and traditions of the past.

In all of these points, however, it must be said again, the question is not simply of grounding ethics in the will of God, but of how God's will is seen as related to man, to the world, to evil. As was said before, 'If ethics is understood in terms of a relationship to God, then everything depends on how that relationship is understood.'

# II

# Ethical Commentary and Political Decision

## DAVID MARTIN

The purpose of this short paper is twofold. It aims to comment on the morality of corporate bodies, in particular that of church or state, in so far as they deliver themselves on the ethical aspects of political decisions. (These are not the only corporate bodies which might be discussed: trades unions also come in the same category.) It also aims to compare and contrast the role of ethical commentary performed on behalf of a corporate body like the church with the role of the actual decision-maker. In other words, I am discussing the general difference between corporate morality (whether in church or in state) and individual morality in so far as it relates to the further difference between commentator and performer, political moralist and politician. The argument is going to be that all corporate morality, whether it consists in political moralizing by a church or in political decisions claiming some ethical justification on the part of the state, tends to lay its stress on consequences. That being so it introduces a strong empirical element in the form of scientific predictions about the likely consequences of alternative policies. This empirical element will be economically labelled sociology. And it is sociology which may perhaps enable us to locate the difference between ethical commentary and political decision, since it can contrast the type of consequence which concerns the commentator with the type which concerns the politician – and also indicate perhaps the extent to which they must overlap. The argument just set out must now be presented in more extended fashion, beginning with the point made about the estimation of consequences.

One of the major traditions of ethical reflection lays its prime

stress on the consequences of acts rather than on their intrinsic
nature or on the motives lying behind them. No doubt it is true that
a stress on the intrinsic qualities of actions hardly avoids some calcu-
lation of consequences just as a stress on the consequences of actions
must include some estimation of the intrinsic worth of particular
sets of consequences when weighed against other sets. Nevertheless,
I hope the broad distinction still holds. At any rate I presume there
is agreement on the supposition that whatever the emphasis of
different ethical traditions they all must concern themselves with
consequences to some extent.

It seems to me that a shift of emphasis occurs when the focus of
concern moves from individual to corporate ethics. Presumably
there is less interest in the *motives* of an action: whether or not, for
example, the intentions of an ecclesiastical or political agency were
good. And so far as the contrast between intrinsic and consequential
is concerned I suppose that not only is a stress on the consequences
of a decision so much the greater but that the main attention is on
the ability of whole *sets* of decisions when integrated together to
produce an approved state of affairs. Thus the primary questions
turn on an organized relation between whole ranges of decisions
and recommendations and an envisaged condition of communal
well-being.

If this is the case – and I make all these suggestions with extreme
diffidence having regard for the immense complexities involved –
then the science of social consequences, sociology, comes to play an
even greater role in the decisions of corporate bodies and in the
ethical commentary made by one corporate body on the decisions of
another.

There is no difficulty in stating how sociology enters into the
decisions of corporate bodies. It can provide social information, and
set the context of a problem. It can, at least in principle, estimate
the likely results if course (*a*) is followed rather than course (*b*). It
can bring within the scope of intentionality what previously might
have been the unintended consequences of action. And, finally, it is
capable of tracing the antecedents of a situation, a peculiarly
important function so far as ethical commentary is concerned and
one which raises some profound problems. These services which
'sociology' may provide represent the combined resources of economics, political science, etc., and are only new in that nowadays
such services are explicitly sought and are systematically performed.

Presumably in the past every politician and ethical commentator was an amateur political scientist and economist, more explicitly perhaps after Machiavelli in the European experience but implicitly everywhere and at all times. What is now understood in the multi-dimensional perspectives of sociology as systematized, verified propositional knowledge has always been practical knowledge, even if working with a 'Ptolemaic' rather than a 'Copernican' perspective.

I take it there is no dispute about the relevance of this type of information in shaping ethical commentary and political decision.[1] I am not saying, of course, that such information and such predictions enter into the ethical substance so as to leap over the chasm between is (was or will be) and ought. However, there is an important aspect worth noting just at this point and it relates not to 'is' and 'ought' but to 'ought' and 'can'. To some extent ethical commentary can only say that a politician should do thus and thus if it can be shown that it was possible for him to do so. Sociology provides an analysis of practical limits in given situations and to that extent restricts the range of justifiable free-ranging finger-wagging. And of course to the extent that it shows an action as part of a whole *system* with a particular 'drift' then ethical commentary shifts away from particular actions to discuss a whole system of relationships, a whole history of tendencies, a whole semi-determinate course of likelihoods.[2] This is a complex point which must be taken up below since it relates to the degree to which ethical commentary may take up alternative perspectives outside the 'system', how far such alternative perspectives need to represent a genuine empirical likelihood (or at least possibility) and how far *back* the tracing of a history of tendencies should go – inasmuch as the last Conservative government is too near and Adam too far.

I hope I have begun to indicate how sociology can enter into ethical commentary and the kind of problems it raises. If so I can now move on to my contrast and comparison between ethical commentary and political decision. The appropriate point at which to begin is one which least illustrates the difference and which also most brings out the element of the intrinsic as distinct from the consequential. Commentators and politicians alike agree in being against sin and on the side of the angels. Actually, to say that everybody is against sin is somewhat of a rhetorical exaggeration since in situations which are sufficiently crucial most moralists and actors agree that ends justify means. They apologize, maybe, for violence, falsehood and promise-breaking but argue that such things are necessary in the circumstances. But at any rate they very seldom apply this argument to those of their opponents who utilize the same escape clause. Moreover, those who regard any means as justified usually adopt the attitude of moral scold towards their enemies.

Clearly sociology is not relevant to a basic evaluation of truth-telling, promise-keeping, etc., though it might provide an estimate as to the point where things had so deteriorated that one had to utilize the moral escape-hatch: as regards truth-telling this point of deterioration can be reached very quickly.[3] But sociology is relevant at the next level of commentary and decision, which might most usefully be illustrated by the proposition that colour, race and religion are irrelevant. As regards the point about the irrelevance of colour and race, sociology can usually erode racist arguments in their empirical form though clearly not in the form of a basic attitude towards blackness or colour. On the other hand it can replace the false arguments about inferior moral and intellectual qualities by much more plausible arguments regarding tolerable degrees of cultural heterogeneity. As regards the point about religion the same argument based on cultural heterogeneity holds, and sociology could obviously bolster a position which stated communal peace as an overall aim and predicted that a given degree of religious heterogeneity would lead to an intolerable degree of disruption.

In this area of discussion one has left behind the level of immutable principles and entered the murky level of compromises, varied estimates of likely tendencies, calculations of ultimate and immediate political benefit or popularity, and so on. Presumably it is here that the difference between ethical commentary and political decision can emerge. As I attempt to delineate these differences I shall use language favouring the politician. This is not because I wish to support state rather than church, but because there is at large in our society, particularly on its leftward margins, a form of ethical comment which abuses its advantages and manages to create a false image of moral superiority which a proper disdain for the attractions of office enables it to maintain untarnished. So it seems worth while to set out these advantages in such a way as to be at least fair even to politicians, on the supposition that as individuals they are not inferior to the rest of us, either morally or intellectually. As I do this some of the advantages listed may seem to be incidental, others more inherent in the whole mode of ethical comment, but I shall not attempt to differentiate between them.

In the first place ethical commentary can afford to restate first principles when politicians are already lost in the quagmire of compromises and would rather not hear about such things. It can point out that the colour *is* irrelevant, the promise breaking *is* improper and so on. An allied advantage, which is in a sense the reverse side of the coin, consists in the ability to admit that first principles are *continually* broken, whereas politicians pretend this only occurs under pressure of the direst necessity. Ethical comment can show empirically, for example, that a government has over-extended itself in terms of promises, so that if it keeps one it *must* break another. Or it can show that solemn pledges are made with unstated reservations about 'vital interests' (variously defined) on the part of participants, and that the solemnities are to some extent a kind of mutually deceptive confidence trick which is also for the benefit of dangerous third parties. In other words comment can be both more naïvely moral than politicians and more sophisticatedly honest about the actual processes involved. Both possibilities are immensely satisfying to their practitioners.

Comment can ignore survival as a primary value, a point related to the issue of 'vital interests' just raised. It need not think in terms of party survival or national survival, whereas a politician must think in terms of both. And if one can ignore survival one can also ignore immediate and ultimate electoral considerations, the appropriate garnishing of images, the buying-off of crucial pressure groups and so on. Indeed, comment can ignore the sometimes mendacious demands of the great democracy to which politicians must at least pretend to give ear. One further refinement open to ethical commentators is the offering of morally prestigious advice in the sure and certain hope that it will not be taken.

However, although the commentating role can ignore the more restricting types of empirical consideration forcing themselves on politicians, yet presumably it must in turn recommend policies or alternative social systems which are empirically viable. The alternatives must be possible and should preferably constitute an option currently open. No doubt social science is relevant to a decision about what is a possible alternative and a genuine immediate option, although this may require precisely that very extensive analysis of the total range of financial and political pressures and historical obligations operating on a government which ethical commentary prefers to avoid. To speak too cautiously within the actual limits of choice gives the politician a chance to avoid a consideration even of possible alternatives. So ethical commentary must not publicly over-prize empirical analysis, otherwise it tends to assimilate its position too closely to that of the decision-maker, thereby losing its impact and relinquishing the essential complementarity of role and division of labour between commentary and political decision. After all, even a clearly unrealistic assessment can *sometimes* help a politician to acquire a little more leeway. However, to perform in this way requires a great deal of empirical political understanding from the commentator, which he often either lacks or does not choose to have.

Another gain of commentary *vis-à-vis* politics is derived from the above and consists in the capacity to ignore opportunity costs. These costs may be immediate or they may be the ultimate opportunity costs of choices between degrees of emphasis on either hierarchy or equality, power or justice, wisdom or democracy.[4]

An empirical situation is the one which confronts a politician *now*, but ethical commentary can say that policy ($y$) would not need to be followed *now* if policy ($x$) had not been implemented in the past. However, although the past can be undone verbally there is a limit on the extent to which it can be undone practically. Moreover, the politician often cannot even undo the past verbally since this would detract from the viability of his current efforts. As noted earlier the commentator must make a choice as to how far he traces back 'bad' decisions and how far he condemns this or that decision as distinct from condemning the system within which they occur.

Finally the commentator has the ability to snipe without revealing his own position in full. A politician is more easily forced to state the criteria with which he is operating with regard to a whole area of politico-ethical discussion whereas the moralist can engage in a moral guerrilla warfare from which he cannot quickly be flushed out.

In sum, I have attempted to show the importance of empirical consequences for both ethical comment and political decision and the difference in mode between the two types of activity. I have further suggested that these differences, where the commentator has the advantage of irresponsibility and the politician the responsibility (not to say consolation) of power, are complementary roles in any politically and morally conscious society. It may be thought immoral or unfair of a commentator to utilize the advantages just outlined, but the alternative is a total assimilation to the considerations most pressing on the actual power holders. It may be that an analysis of empirical pressures and possibilities does lead one logically to such an assimilation, but sociologically it is clear that this course would blacken one's own image, reduce one's impact, and therefore eliminate precisely that element of pressure which one can contribute to a situation – and which is both an additional restriction and an additional freedom for the politician, according to circumstances.[5]

# Notes

### 1. *Some Philosophical Problems in Christian Ethics*

1. A. N. Flew, *God and Philosophy*, Hutchinson 1966, p. 109.

2. P. Nowell-Smith, 'Morality: Religious and Secular', in *Christian Ethics and Contemporary Philosophy*, ed. I. T. Ramsey, SCM Press 1966, pp. 103–8.

3. Commentary, II *Ethics*, lect. 2 (trans. by Thomas Gilby, *St Thomas Aquinas: Philosophical Texts*, OUP 1951, no. 786).

4. K. E. Kirk, *The Threshold of Ethics*, Skeffington 1933, pp. 38f.

5. Paul Ramsey, *Deeds and Rules in Christian Ethics*, 2nd ed., Scribner 1967.

6. The only work known to me that systematically reviews Christian ethics in the light of the main schools of moral philosophy is G. F. Thomas, *Christian Ethics and Moral Philosophy* (Scribner 1955, new ed. 1973), a book which is, in my opinion, the best single survey of Christian ethics and of the philosophical problems that the subject raises.

7. It must be stressed that theological naturalism is a departure from the classical tradition of Christian philosophy and theology.

8. For a persuasive presentation of the view that Christian ethics implies moral objectivity see Keith Ward, *Ethics and Christianity*, Allen and Unwin 1970.

### 2. *Ought and Is*

1. David Hume, *A Treatise of Human Nature* III, 1.1 (ed. A. Selby Bigge, Oxford 1888, p. 469).

2. R. C. Mortimer, *The Elements of Moral Theology*, A. and C. Black 1947, e.g. p. 8.

3. G. E. M. Anscombe, 'Modern Moral Philosophy', *Philosophy* 33, 1958, p. 3.

4. A. C. MacIntyre, 'Hume on "is" and "ought" ' in *The Is/Ought Question*, ed. W. D. Hudson, Macmillan 1969, pp. 35–50.

5. Ronald Atkinson, *Sexual Morality*, Hutchinson 1965, p. 18.

6. R. M. Hare, 'Descriptivism', Annual Philosophical Lecture, *Proceedings of the British Academy* 49, 1963, p. 115.

7. Jonathan Harrison, 'When is a Principle a Moral Principle?', *Proceedings of the Aristotelian Society, Supplementary Volume (PASS)* 28, 1954, p. 120.

8. P. R. Foot, 'Moral Arguments', *Mind* 67, 1958, p. 507.

9. *Concise Encyclopaedia of Western Philosophy and Philosophers*, ed. J. O. Urmson, Hutchinson 1960, p. 139.

10. D. Emmet, *Rules, Roles and Relations*, Macmillan 1966, ch. III.

11. Ibid., p. 47; see also pp. 52–5.

12. Ibid., p. 39.

13. Ibid., p. 15.

14. Atkinson, *Sexual Morality*, p. 29.

15. E.g., D. Emmet, op. cit., pp. 19ff.; Paul Halmos, *The Faith of the Counsellors*, Constable 1966.

16. As witness Hare's careful recognition of the 'descriptive meaning' of evaluative terms, e.g. in *Freedom and Reason*, OUP 1963, p. 21.

17. Quoted by Hare in *The Language of Morals*, OUP 1952, p. 79. Likewise the *Shorter Oxford English Dictionary* has 'a term of general or indefinite commendation'. The dictionary-makers appear to let Professor Hare down in the *Concise* version of the *OED*. Here 'commending' is no longer taken as central, though 'commendable' figures (after 'Having the right qualities, satisfactory, adequate' and before 'morally excellent, virtuous') in a long list of synonyms and examples. However, there is still no infringement of 'non-naturalism': the terms taken as synonyms are themselves 'evaluative', and indeed 'having the right qualities' could conveniently introduce us to Professor Hare's key concept of *choice*. There is no heinous slide to 'commendable' from 'commended'.

18. E.g. Jonathan Harrison, *PASS* 1954, p. 116: 'Moral principles are not something we make, but something we discover.'

P. R. Foot, *Mind* 67, 1958, p. 505: 'A man can no more decide for himself what is evidence for rightness and wrongness than he can decide what is evidence for monetary inflation or a tumour on the brain.'

J. N. Findlay, *Values and Intentions*, Allen and Unwin 1961, p. 24, makes the distinction between deciding *that* and deciding *to*, pointing out that the former involves submission to fixed canons of settlement. 'Our "values" are the relatively fixed points of the compass by means of which our choices are guided: it makes no sense to speak of arbitrarily choosing them.'

J. Benson, 'The Characterisation of Actions and the Virtuous Agent', *Proceedings of the Aristotelian Society (PAS)* NS 63, 1962–63, p. 260: 'A man cannot please himself about what is to constitute a moral consideration.'

R. Bambrough, 'Praising with Faint Damns', *Religion and Humanism*, BBC 1964, p. 72: 'Sartre is right about the complexity of moral choice; but he is wrong to the point of being irresponsible when he goes on to preach *commitment*, to suggest that we may freely fashion our values because they are so difficult to find.'

C. C. W. Taylor, reviewing *Freedom and Reason* in *Mind* 74, 1965, p. 280, suggests that Professor Hare's view 'appears quite opposed to the moral consciousness of the ordinary man, who is apt to take it for granted that from the fact that an action has such and such characteristics it follows that it is right or wrong'.

G. Warnock, *Contemporary Moral Philosophy*, Macmillan 1967, p. 47: 'Hare . . . is saying, not only that it is for us to decide what our moral opinions are, but also that it is for us to decide what to take as grounds for or against any moral opinion. . . . I do not, it seems, decide that flogging is wrong because I *am* against cruelty; rather, I decide that flogging is wrong because I *decide to be* against cruelty. . . . But such a person, surely, is not so much a model as a menace.'

D. Pole, 'On Practical Reason and Benevolence', *PAS* NS 68, 1967–1968, p. 132: 'In place of intuition Hare offers something called "decision"; which I for my part find far more mysterious, for I never consciously took such a decision – that is, a "decision of principle" (though, of course, I have often decided practical issues, decided not on, but in the light of principles).'

*The Jerusalem Bible*, Darton, Longman and Todd 1966, note on Gen. 2.17: 'This knowledge (sc. of good and evil) is a privilege which God reserves to himself and which man, by sinning, is to lay hands on, 3.5, 22. Hence it does not mean omniscience, which fallen man does not possess; nor is it moral discrimination, for unfallen man already had it and God could not refuse it to a rational being. It is the power of deciding for himself what is good and what is evil and of acting accordingly, a claim to complete moral independence by which man refuses to recognise his status as a created being. The first sin was an attack on God's sovereignty, a sin of pride.' (Cf. John Baker, *The Foolishness of God*, Darton, Longman and Todd 1970, p. 36.)

19. G. E. M. Anscombe, *Intention*, Blackwell 1957, p. 70.
20. Ibid. See also P. R. Foot, 'Goodness and Choice', *PASS* 35, 1961, pp. 55ff.
21. R. M. Hare, 'Descriptivism', p. 125.
22. E.g. P. R. Foot, *PASS*, 1961, pp. 46f.
23. G. E. Moore, *Principia Ethica*, CUP 1903, ch. IV.
24. R. W. Hepburn, *Christianity and Paradox*, C. and A. Watts 1958, ch. VIII.
25. I have tried to explain such a way of speaking in *The Character of Christian Morality*, Faith Press 1965, ch. IV (2nd ed. forthcoming).
26. 'Descriptivism', p. 130.
27. Ibid., p. 126.
28. Cf. A. R. Montefiore, 'Goodness and Choice', *PASS* 35, 1961, p. 65; also David Pole, *PAS*, 1967–8, p. 139.
29. There is a parallel here with the question of 'the ethics of belief' and the special senses in which people can be said to choose what to believe. One can put oneself in a position where one will be more likely

to come to want, or believe, such and such. One might have a responsibility for doing this; but one is not exactly choosing such wants or beliefs.

30. To work this view out fully one would need to know in what sense animals can have purposes and how they could be related to human morality.

31. See John MacMurray *The Self as Agent*, Faber 1957; also e.g. Stuart Hampshire, *Thought and Action*, Chatto and Windus 1959. Since writing the above paragraph I have elaborated upon it in *Incarnation and Immanence*, Hodder and Stoughton 1973.

32. P. R. Foot, *Mind* 67, 1958, p. 510.

33. Ps. 16. I have gone into this somewhat further in 'Christian Flourishing', *Religious Studies* 5, 1969, pp. 167-8 (to be reprinted in *The Character of Christian Morality*, 2nd ed.).

34. See in particular: G. F. Woods, 'Natural Law and Christian Ethics', *Theology* LXVIII, 1965, reprinted as ch. 4 below; H. L. A. Hart, *The Concept of Law*, OUP 1961, p. 176 and ch. 9. Professor Woods, having shown himself well aware of the difficulties, was able all the more tellingly to point out the large areas of agreement about 'human nature' which do exist, e.g. in conceptions such as 'human rights' or 'mature, balanced and wholesome personality'. Professor Hart has shown that such agreement is indeed not surprising since certain 'truisms' about what people are like enable one to specify a 'minimum content of natural law'.

35. See Alexander Macbeath, *Experiments in Living*, Macmillan 1952.

36. See Hart, op. cit.; John Lucas, *The Principles of Politics*, Clarendon Press 1966, e.g. Section 1.

37. Cf. P. R. Foot, *Mind* 67, 1958, pp. 512f.; Advisory Council for the Church's Ministry, *Teaching Christian Ethics*, SCM Press 1974, pp. 52f.

38. ' "Damage" includes death, injury, delay, loss or other damage of whatsoever nature'; from 'Conditions of Contract', in a BEA passenger ticket.

39. Cf. John Lucas, *The Principle of Politics*, p. 173.

40. Cf. P. R. Foot, *Mind* 67, 1958, p. 571.

41. E.g. *Sexual Morality*, pp. 64f., 181f. See also *Towards a Quaker View of Sex*, Friends Home Service Committee 1963.

42. Bishop Butler, *Dissertation on the Nature of Virtue*, § 13.

43. *Thought and Action*, p. 236. Cf. G. J. Warnock, *Contemporary Moral Philosophy*, p. 67.

44. H. P. Owen; see p. 9 above.

45. *Rules, Role and Relations*, p. 178. Cf. G. E. M. Anscombe, *Intention*, p. 74.

46. Cf. Professor Hare, in *Theories of Ethics*, ed. P. R. Foot, OUP 1967, p. 82. 'If Geach wants to make it possible to draw from the meaning of "man" conclusions about what is contrary to or conducive to a man's being a good man . . . he will, in short, have to make "man" into a functional word.'

47. Professor Hare well says, *Language of Morals*, p. 128, that 'We only have standards for a class of objects' when there are or might be occasions of choice. But if I understand him rightly he slides away from the concept of 'choosing a man' to the different concept of what a man would choose: 'We should not speak of good men unless we had the choice, what sort of men to try to become' (ibid.). Similarly on p. 141: 'We get stirred up about the goodness of men because we are men.' This seems to ignore our relationships with other people whose goodness matters to us quite as much as our own. We do not get stirred up about the goodness of chronometers, not only because we cannot turn into chronometers, but because after all chronometers do not matter to us nearly as much as human beings do.

48. 'Descriptivism', p. 126.

49. I have argued this point further in *Incarnation and Immanence*, pp. 185ff.

50. *Christianity and Paradox*, pp. 151–4.

51. *The Language of Morals*, p. 69. Cf. C. C. W. Taylor, *Mind* 74, 1965, p. 297, reviewing *Freedom and Reason*.

52. A. Clutton Brock, 'A Dream of Heaven' in B. H. Streeter et al., *Immortality*, Macmillan 1917, p. 225.

53. *The Language of Morals*, p. 142.

54. *Mind*, 1958, p. 509. Cf. G. J. Warnock, *Contemporary Moral Philosophy*, p. 68.

55. Cf. M. Tanner, 'Examples in Moral Philosophy', *PAS* NS 65, 1964–65, p. 73: ' "Naturalism" only *has* triumphed . . . if it can be extended to the most general moral terms.'

56. St Augustine, *Confessions* I.1.

57. *Law and Love*, Faith Press 1962, p. 82.

## 3. *Nature and Morality*

1. *A fortiori* it is impossible to deduce moral principles from the facts of *sub*-human nature. On this impossibility see the chapter entitled *Naturam Sequere* in Basil Willey, *The English Moralists*, Chatto and Windus 1964.

2. For such agreement between different cultures in both the ancient and the modern world see an appendix to C. S. Lewis's (unjustly neglected) *The Abolition of Man*, OUP 1943, and S. C. Thakur's *Christian and Hindu Ethics*, Allen and Unwin 1969. At the same time many modern writers claim that the important element in the idea of natural law is its *form* (as a distinctive and obligatory principle); they are ready to concede that its essential and unvarying *content* consists in a few, highly general, principles. (See, e.g., Columba Ryan's contribution to *Light on the Natural Law*, ed. Illtud Evans, Burns and Oates 1965.)

3. Its most obvious formulation is in the concept of 'natural rights' – that is, rights which inhere in the nature of man as such. It is significant how often individuals and nations profess subscription to these rights

even when they cannot give them any metaphysical justification, and even when they violate them in practice.

4. A. M. Farrer, 'Examination of Theological Belief', in *Faith and Logic*, ed. Basil Mitchell, Allen and Unwin 1957, p. 29.

5. J. H. Jacques, *The Right and the Wrong*, SPCK 1965, pp. 48–9.

6. I. T. Ramsey, 'Moral Judgments and God's Commands', *Christian Ethics and Contemporary Philosophy*, SCM Press 1966, p. 162. He is here commenting on R. M. Hare. Cf. his comments on H. L. A. Hart's theory of natural law, 'Towards a Rehabilitation of Natural Law', ibid., p. 389.

7. W. D. Hudson, *Ethical Intuitionism*, Macmillan 1967, p. 166.

8. Some of the tests for moral intuition are stated by A. C. Ewing in his *Ethics*, English Universities Press 1967, pp. 131–4.

9. See E. Kamenka, *Marxism and Ethics*, Macmillan 1969.

10. A. G. N. Flew, *Evolutionary Ethics*, Macmillan 1967.

11. D. J. O'Connor, *Aquinas and Natural Law*, Macmillan 1967. pp. 83f.

12. C. S. Lewis, *Mere Christianity*, Fontana 1955, p. 28.

13. H. McCabe, *Law, Love and Language*, Sheed and Ward 1968.

14. Op. cit., pp. 6of., 94f., 100–2.

15. W. D. Hudson, 'Fact and Moral Value', *Religious Studies* 5, 1969, pp. 133f.

16. Paul Helm, 'Fact and Moral Value – a Comment on Dr Hudson's Paper', ibid., p. 143.

17. A. D. Galloway, 'Fact and Value in Theological Ethics', ibid., p. 176.

## 4. *Natural Law and Christian Ethics:*

### *A Comment from the Reformed Tradition*

1. Calvin, *Institutes of the Christian Religion*, IV. xx. 14.

2. Ibid., IV. xx. 16.

3. Quoted by Heinz Zahrnt, *The Question of God*, Eng. trs., Collins 1969, p. 147.

4. I.e., duty to God and neighbour, or only to neighbour.

5. Cf. E. Brunner, *The Divine Imperative*, Eng. trs., Lutterworth Press 1937, p. 232.

6. See e.g. encyclical letter, *Humanae Vitae*, 4: 'It is, in fact, indisputable, as Our Predecessors have many times declared, that Jesus Christ, when communicating to Peter and to the Apostles His divine authority and sending them to teach all nations His commandments, constituted them as guardians and authentic interpreters of all the moral law, not only, that is, of the law of the gospel, but also of the natural law, which is also an expression of the will of God, the faithful fulfilment of which is equally necessary for salvation.' (Quoted from Leo Pyle, ed., *Pope and Pill*, Darton, Longman and Todd 1968, p. 240.)

7. Ronald Atkinson, *Sexual Morality*, Hutchinson 1965, p. 34.

8. See the essay 'Ought and Is', ch. 2 above, and E. Schillebeeckx, *God the Future of Man*, Eng. trs., Sheed and Ward 1969, pp. 194ff.

9. P. Lehmann, *Ethics in a Christian Context*, SCM Press 1963, p. 101.

10. W. A. Visser 't Hooft and J. H. Oldham, eds, *The Church and its Function in Society*, Allen and Unwin 1937, p. 210. The concept of the middle axiom has been used more in the United States, through the work of John Bennett, than in Britain, though William Temple used the idea at the Malvern Conference, and in 1942–44 the Church of Scotland actually formulated some middle axioms to guide the political thinking and decisions of Christians in the post-war years. The proposals were contained in the Reports of a special Commission of the General Assembly, under the convenership of Dr John Baillie.

### *A Comment from the Roman Catholic Tradition*

1. Cf. ch. 5 below, 'The Natural Law and the Law of Christ'.

2. Cf. E. McDonagh, 'Discerning God's Action in the World', *Theology* LXXV, 1972, pp. 451–62.

### 5. *The Natural Law and the Law of Christ*

1. E. McDonagh, ed., *Moral Theology Renewed*, Papers of the Maynooth Union Summer School 1964, Gill, Dublin, 1965.

2. Cf. C. H. Dodd, *Gospel and Law*, CUP 1951.

3. B. Schüller, *Gesetz und Freiheit*, Patmos-Verlag, Dusseldorf, 1966.

4. F. Böckle, ed., *Das Naturrecht im Disput*, Patmos-Verlag, Dusseldorf, 1966, pp. 127ff.

5. E. McDonagh, 'Penance and Charity' in *Sin and Repentance*, Papers of the Maynooth Union Summer School 1966, ed. D. O. Callaghan, Gill, Dublin, 1967.

6. K. Rahner, 'The "Commandment" of Love in relation to the other Commandments', *Theological Investigations* V, Eng. trs., Darton, Longman and Todd 1966, pp. 439–59.

7. This I have more fully developed in a paper entitled 'The Christian Ethic: A Community Ethic', in E. McDonagh, *Invitation and Response*, Gill and Macmillan, Dublin, 1972, pp. 38–58.

8. For moral theology one of the most important themes of contemporary theology is the eschatological orientation of Christian life. Cf. J. Moltmann, *Theology of Hope*, Eng. trs., SCM Press 1967; J. B. Metz, *Theology of the World*, Eng. trs., Burns and Oates 1969.

9. Gal. 6.3. It became common usage in the current renewal of moral theology with the publication of B. Häring, *Das Gesetz Christi*, Wewel, Freiburg i. Br., 1954, 8th ed. 1967 (Eng. trs. of vol. I, *The Law of Christ*, Mercier Press, Cork, 1961).

10. *Summa Theologica* I.II. 106.1.

11. Ibid.

12. Rom. 8.15.

13. J. Fuchs, *Moral und Moraltheologie nach dem Konzil*, Herder, Freiburg i. Br., 1967, pp. 94ff.

14. F. Böckle, loc. cit.

15. This is argued very effectively, although in different terms, by B. Schüller, 'Wie weit kann die Moraltheologie das Naturrecht entbehren?', *Lebendiges Zeugnis*, 1965, pp. 41–65.

16. F. Böckle, loc. cit.; J. Fuchs, *Natural Law*, Eng. trs., Gill, Dublin, 1965, pp. 6ff.

### 6. *The Bible and Christian Ethics*

1. *Von Reimarus zu Wrede*, Tübingen 1906; Eng. trs., A. and C. Black 1910, 3rd ed., 1954.

### 7. *How we make Moral Decisions*

1. Joseph Butler, *Fifteen Sermons*, 1726, Preface.

2. David Hume, *An Enquiry Concerning the Principles of Morals*, 1751, Sect. 1 (Selby-Bigge edn., § 138).

3. John Stuart Mill, *Utilitarianism*, 1863, ch. IV.

### 8. *God and Morality*

1. A. C. Ewing, 'The Autonomy of Ethics', in *Prospect for Metaphysics*, ed. I. T. Ramsey, Allen and Unwin 1961.

2. C. H. Dodd, *Gospel and Law*, CUP 1951.

3. I John 4.7–21.

4. See Barnabas Lindars in the next chapter.

5. Matt. 5.48.

6. See E. J. Tinsley, *The Imitation of God in Christ*, SCM Press 1960.

7. Studied in H. H. Price, *Belief*, Allen and Unwin 1969.

8. Richard Robinson, *An Atheist's Values*, OUP 1964, p. 157.

9. P. F. Strawson, 'Social Morality and Individual Ideal', in *Christian Ethics and Contemporary Philosophy*, ed. I. T. Ramsey, SCM Press 1966, pp. 280–98.

10. G. R. Grice, *The Grounds of Moral Judgement*, CUP 1967.

### 9. *Imitation of God and Imitation of Christ*

1. E. J. Tinsley, *The Imitation of God in Christ*, SCM Press 1960.

2. In his article 'Imitation of Christ' in *A Dictionary of Christian Ethics*, ed. J. Macquarrie, SCM Press 1967, p. 163, Tinsley does not consider the question of the imitation of God, and so avoids the pitfalls considered in this paper.

3. Cf. G. Fohrer, 'Die Vorgeschichte Israels im Lichte neuer Quellen', *Studien zur alttestamentliche Theologie und Geschichte (1949–1966)* (Beiheft zur *Zeitschrift für die alttestamentliche Wissenschaft* 115), 1969, pp. 297–308.

4. Cf. the texts from Ras Shamra translated by G. R. Driver, *Canaanite Myths and Legends*, T. and T. Clark 1956.

5. It is mentioned as a possibility by D. W. Thomas, 'Some Unusual Ways of Expressing the Superlative', *Vetus Testamentum* 3, 1953, pp. 209–14.

6. For the whole question, cf. A. C. Charity, *Events and their After-life*, CUP 1967.

## 10. *Protestant Ethics and the Will of God*

1. Paul Lehmann, *Ethics in a Christian Context*, SCM Press 1963, p. 76.

2. John Calvin, *Institutes of the Christian Religion*, III. xxiii. 2.

3. Ibid., II. vii. 12.

4. Ibid., III. vii. 1.

5. Ibid.

6. E. Brunner, *The Divine Imperative*, Eng. trs., Lutterworth Press 1937, p. 56.

7. Ibid., p. 53.

8. K. Barth, *Church Dogmatics* II. 2, Eng. trs., T. and T. Clark 1957, p. 536.

9. Brunner, op. cit., p. 111.

10. K. Barth, *The Humanity of God*, Eng. trs., Collins, 1961, p. 85.

11. Brunner, op. cit., p. 71.

12. D. Bonhoeffer, *No Rusty Swords*, Eng. trs., Collins 1965, pp. 43–4, 46.

13. See A. P. d'Entrèves, *Natural Law*, Hutchinson 1951, p. 64; H. P. Owen, 'Some Philosophical Problems in Christian Ethics', ch. 1 above.

14. See e.g. I Samuel 15.

15. Quoted in H. Heppe, *Reformed Dogmatics*, Eng. trs., Allen and Unwin 1950, pp. 97–8.

16. K. Barth, *Church Dogmatics*, II. 2, p. 557.

17. P. H. Nowell-Smith, *Ethics*, Penguin 1954, p. 192.

18. Mr Peter Geach, however, maintains that to ask 'Why should I obey God's Law?' 'is really an insane question'. 'A defiance of an Almighty God is insane . . .' *God and the Soul*, Routledge and Kegan Paul 1969, p. 126.

19. J. Fletcher, *Situation Ethics*, SCM Press 1966, p. 69.

20. J. S. Mill, *Utilitarianism*, Everyman ed., 1910, p. 16.

21. P. Lehmann, op. cit., p. 101 et passim.

22. J. H. Oldham, *The Church and its Function in Society*, Allen and Unwin 1937, p. 235.

23. Ibid., p. 236.

24. Ibid., pp. 236–7.

25. D. Bonhoeffer, op. cit., p. 41.

26. Keith Ward in *Ethics and Christianity*, Allen and Unwin 1970, has given a persuasive argument for holding that the moral demand 'is

most adequately characterized in the personalistic language of objective moral purpose, "the will of God" ' (p. 110), and for the complementarity of the models of God as ground of values and as loving and gracious Father.

27. The phrase is J. Fletcher's, op. cit., p. 95.

28. Rom. 12.2 (*NEB*).

29. The 'painter-analogy' has been extensively discussed in some of the papers in Part IV of the volume *Christian Ethics and Contemporary Philosophy*, ed. I. T. Ramsey, SCM Press 1966, but more in terms of creativity than of discernment.

30. E. Brunner, op. cit., p. 73.

## 11. *Ethical Commentary and Political Decision*

1. Perhaps I may anticipate one criticism in so far as I am discussing two out of a possible four boxes, as shown by the following diagram:

|  | *State* | *Other Organizations* |
|---|---|---|
| Action | X |  |
| Ethical Talk |  | X |

I have omitted the two unmarked boxes.

If this were a more extended piece I should no doubt have to consider the restrictions which operate not only on the 'politicians' in the state but those operating on 'politicians' in other organizations (e.g. unions) and the ethical commentary to which they in turn are subject, both within and outside their organizations. Pressure groups like unions are usually restricted by their material interest and by an external ethical commentary based on notions like the rules of the game and the 'national interest'. Pressure groups whose primary *raison d'être* is a critique of a given political system achieve much higher degrees of freedom, and need consider only their own internal cohesion. They have no responsibilities outside their critique, except of course that once they try *effective* political action they must consider tactics in relation to activities which could prove counter-productive, and this consideration of tactics often eventually reacts back to modify their philosophical strategy. The church lies between these two positions, having both material interests (usually) and philosophical strategy. Its critical perspective is restricted by opinion within its constituency (impact depends on representing *somebody*) and the degree of integration it hopes to maintain with other sub-sections of society (e.g. the education system).

2. No doubt one can still say that, given the 'system' and its tendencies, nevertheless politician *x* could have done better than he did.

3. As R. Aron has pointed out (*Eighteen Lectures on Industrial*

*Society*, Weidenfeld and Nicolson 1967), all democratic societies are bound to be hypocritical.

4. Cf. Aron, op. cit., ch. 4, for a discussion of these basic political dilemmas.

5. As an example, one could cite Lloyd George secretly asking to be attacked by newspaper commentators when at Versailles so as to give him more elbow-room at the conference table.

# Index of Subjects

# Index of Names